# The I ♥ TRADER JOE'S® AIR FRYER COOKBOOK

**150 Delicious Recipes Using Foods
from the World's Greatest Grocery Store**

## RITA MOCK-PIKE

Published by:
Ulysses Press
PO Box 3440
Berkeley, CA 94703
www.ulyssespress.com

ISBN: 978-1-64604-322-4
Library of Congress Control Number: 2021946381

Printed in China
10 9 8 7 6 5 4 3 2

Acquisitions editor: Kierra Sondereker
Managing editor: Claire Chun
Editor: Renee Rutledge
Proofreader: Michele Anderson
Interior design and layout: what!design @ whatweb.com
Production: Yesenia Garcia Lopez
Artwork: shutterstock.com

# CONTENTS

## Chapter 4

## DID SOMEBODY SAY SALAD?............................ 65

## Chapter 5

## SEAFOOD SAVORIES ................................... 79

## Chapter 6

## MEAT ME AT THE FAIR................................. 97

## Chapter 7

# THOSE FOWL CHOICES . . . . . . . . . . . . . . . . . . . . . . . . 121

## Chapter 8

# VEGAN-FRIENDLY VICTUALS . . . . . . . . . . . . . . . . . . . 139

## Chapter 9

# BREAKFAST IS FOR WINNERS. . . . . . . . . . . . . . . . . . . 155

# INTRODUCTION

Growing up in the kitchen with Jerrie Mock, first woman to fly solo around the world and gourmet chef used to entertaining princes, ambassadors, and other foreign dignitaries, I've seen a world—literally!—of cooking styles and flavor combinations. Grandma Jerrie passed away before a Trader Joe's opened up in Tallahassee, where she retired, but let me tell you this: she would have killed for the opportunity to visit the fabulous store.

Now, carrying on her tradition of worldwide cuisine, I love the choices that Trader Joe's offers for super-easy "fixes" for recipes I can't otherwise garner ingredients for. The premade spice blends like Furikake make ramen soups a snap—and the 21 Seasoning Salute blend for seafood is an instant win.

For me, Trader Joe's makes my love of entertaining with elegant (and easy!) dishes so much easier. The cultivated collections, the frozen veggies, the premium sauces at a budget-friendly price all make my ever-busy kitchen a happy place.

Now add in the wonder of the air fryer—a gift from my mother-in-law I couldn't have guessed would save my culinary butt—has made all the Trader Joe's ingredients I love so much even better.

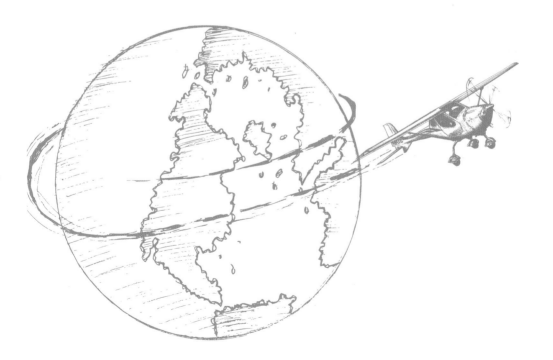

# Chapter 1

# APPS HERE, PLEASE

# SPICY TJ'S FALAFEL

*Falafel is one of those foods that hits all the marks—vegan, gluten-free, dairy-free, and utterly delicious. Plus, it's a fairly familiar food, so even those guests who may not be keen on the "frees" of the food will enjoy it without questioning why you're making it for them. And with this particular recipe, using TJ's premade falafel, the spiciness of the Ajika spice blend really ups the game for these tasty "Mediterranean hush puppies."*

**1 (12-ounce) package Trader Joe's Fully Cooked Falafel, frozen**

**olive oil cooking spray**

**1 tablespoon Trader Joe's Ajika Georgian Seasoning Blend**

**Trader Joe's Tzatziki Creamy Garlic Cucumber Dip (optional)**

**YIELD: 4 SERVINGS**

Set your air fryer to 375°F and preheat for 5 minutes. Grab a plastic container with a lid and dump the bag of falafel into the container. Gently coat the falafel with olive oil spray and put the lid on. Shake thoroughly to coat everything with the spray—adding more, if needed. Then add the Ajika spice blend, cover again, and shake, coating the falafel with the spices.

Pour the falafel into the air fryer basket and cook for 10 minutes. Remove the basket, shake the falafel around, repositioning them—or, if they're not turning easily on their own, use tongs to flip them. Then return the basket and cook for another 5 to 10 minutes, until they're hot all the way through. Let stand for 5 minutes and serve plain or with tzatziki, if using.

**PREP TIME:** 3 minutes
**COOK TIME:** 15 to 20 minutes
**TOTAL TIME:** 18 to 23 minutes

# ROASTED ARTICHOKE POPPERS

*Artichoke hearts may not be the first thing that comes to mind as "poppers"—especially without that typical breading, but these come "ready" from TJ's for the perfect easy nibbles with little time and effort involved. Add the right dipping sauce and you'll even get the veggie-adverse to pop 'em in.*

**12 ounces Trader Joe's Artichoke Hearts, frozen**

**olive oil spray**

**ground black pepper, to taste**

**garlic powder, to taste**

**your favorite dipping sauce**

**YIELD: 1 SERVING PER ARTICHOKE**

Preheat the air fryer to 360°F for 5 minutes while you prep the artichoke hearts. Lay out the artichoke hearts on a tray or plate and lightly spray them with olive oil. Next, sprinkle the black pepper and garlic powder over the hearts, to taste. Remove the basket from the air fryer and place the artichoke in the basket, spice-side down. Now spray them again with olive oil and sprinkle again with black pepper and garlic powder. Return the basket to the air fryer and cook the artichokes for 5 minutes. When the timer dings, remove the basket, toss the artichoke hearts gently, and return them to the air fryer. Cook for another 5 to 8 minutes, Remove from the fryer and let them stand for 5 minutes before serving with your favorite dipping sauces.

For the dipping sauce, I highly recommend Tzatziki Creamy Garlic Cucumber Dip, or TJ's Organic Kansas City Style BBQ Sauce.

**PREP TIME:** 5 minutes
**COOK TIME:** 10 to 13 minutes
**TOTAL TIME:** 15 to 18 minutes

# MAPLE BACON-WRAPPED TRADER TOTS

*Maple syrup, bacon, and tater tots? You really can't get any more breakfast-y than that! Nor can you get more delicious. Best part? It's super easy and pretty fast to make them.*

**1 (12-ounce) package Trader Joe's Uncured Apple Smoked Bacon**

**⅓ cup pure maple syrup**

**½ (32-ounce) bag Trader Joe's Trader Potato Tots, frozen**

**YIELD: 10 TO 12 SERVINGS**

Cut the bacon strips in half, lengthwise. Place the raw bacon in a medium bowl with the maple syrup. Make sure each strip gets thoroughly coated with syrup. Leave the bacon to soak while you lay out the potato tots on a baking sheet.

Preheat the air fryer to 400°F. While that's heating up, wrap each tot with a strip of maple-soaked bacon, then return each tot to the baking sheet. Place the bacon-wrapped tots in the air fryer and cook for 15 to 17 minutes, or until the bacon is crisp. About halfway through, using tongs, flip the tots over. When cooked, remove them from the air fryer and let stand 2 to 3 minutes before serving.

**PREP TIME:** 10 minutes
**COOK TIME:** 15 to 20 minutes
**TOTAL TIME:** 25 to 35 minutes

# CRUNCHY ASPARAGUS SPEARS

*My mother was raised on a fruit and vegetable farm—so I've always eaten most varieties of veggies my whole life. A special favorite for me is asparagus. My husband, however, isn't so keen on this stalky veg, so I knew I wanted something he'd enjoy as much as I do. Enter the crunchy asparagus spear! They're like healthy fries and he loves them!*

**12 ounces Trader Joe's Asparagus Spears, frozen**

**olive oil cooking spray**

**ground black pepper, to taste**

**garlic powder, to taste**

**granulated dried onion, to taste**

**YIELD: 4 SERVINGS**

Preheat the air fryer to 350°F for 5 minutes. Lay out the asparagus on plate or cutting board, side by side. Gently mist the spears with olive oil spray and sprinkle seasonings over the spears. Then turn the spears over and repeat the spray-and-sprinkle process.

Place the spears in the air fryer basket, not overlapping. Cook for 8 to 10 minutes. They should be crispy at this point. If they're still a little too soft, cook for 2 more minutes. Then remove them from the basket and let stand for 5 minutes. Serve warm for tasty, crisp spears.

**PREP TIME:** 5 minutes
**COOK TIME:** 8 to 10 minutes
**TOTAL TIME:** 13 to 15 minutes

# PORK GYOZA POTSTICKERS

*Gyoza potstickers are one of the best apps around. So easy, so tasty, so fast. I love serving these at parties and holidays or other special occasions.*

**1 (16-ounce) package Trader Joe's Pork Gyoza Potstickers**

**olive oil spray**

**Trader Ming's Gyoza Dipping Sauce**

**YIELD: 3 TO 4 SERVINGS**

Preheat the air fryer to 400°F for 5 minutes. Lightly spray the basket and add the potstickers, not overlapping. Lightly mist the potstickers, then cook for 3 minutes.

Remove the basket and flip the potstickers, then cook for an additional 2 to 3 minutes. Remove the basket and let them stand for 5 minutes, then serve with Gyoza Dipping Sauce.

**PREP TIME:** 5 minutes
**COOK TIME:** 5 to 6 minutes
**TOTAL TIME:** 10 to 11 minutes

# TZATZIKI STUFFED DOLMA WRAPS

*I first tried dolmas in Greektown in Chicago during my senior year of college. I instantly fell in love. The tangy "something" in these stuffed grape leaves remains one of my favorite treats to this day. The only way I could think to improve them was adding tzatziki and puff pastry. You're welcome.*

**1 (18.3-ounce) package Trader Joe's All Butter Puff Pastry**

**1 (9.86-ounce) can Trader Joe's Quinoa Stuffed Dolmas**

**Trader Joe's Tzatziki Creamy Garlic Cucumber Dip**

**olive oil spray**

**YIELD: 10 WRAPS**

Preheat the air fryer to 375°F. Lay out the puff pastry sheets on a flat surface. Cut the sheets lengthwise into 5 strips per sheet, making sure each strip has about 1 inch extra on each side of a dolma. Flour the surface and roll out slightly to make them large enough for the dolmas. Spread tzatziki on each strip, then place a dolma at one end of each strip. Roll the pastry up, around the dolma, then tuck the ends of the dough over the ends of the dolmas to fully wrap them.

Lightly spray the inside of the air fryer basket with olive oil spray, then place the wraps in the basket, not touching one another. Cook for 10 minutes or until the pastry is golden-brown. Remove the basket from the air fryer and let the wraps cool for 5 to 10 minutes before serving.

**PREP TIME:** 7 minutes
**COOK TIME:** 10 minutes
**TOTAL TIME:** 17 minutes

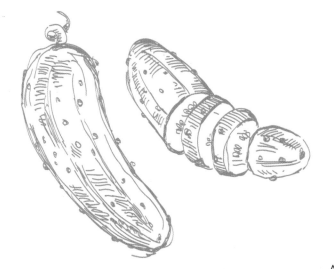

# EASY PIZZA ROLLS

*Who doesn't love pizza bites? And these are so easy and delicious! Just roll out quickly, stuff, fold, and cook in under 10 minutes. They're perfect for parties, after-school snacks, and so much more.*

**16 ounces Trader Giotto's Ready to Bake Garlic & Herb Pizza Dough**

**all-purpose flour, for rolling**

**Trader Giotto's Fat Free Pizza Sauce**

**12 teaspoons shredded mozzarella, divided**

**12 teaspoons chopped pepperoni**

**garlic powder**

**dried oregano**

**crushed red pepper (optional)**

**olive oil spray**

**YIELD: 12 ROLLS**

Separate the pizza dough into 12 evenly sized pieces. Set aside. Lightly flour a surface with all-purpose flour. Take one dough ball and roll out to a disk about ¼-inch thick. Repeat with the other dough balls.

Preheat the air fryer to 400°F for 5 minutes. Arrange the disks on the floured surface. Spread ½ to 1 teaspoon pizza sauce on each disc. Sprinkle a small amount of cheese over the pizza sauce, then add pepperoni pieces. Top with a dash of garlic powder, dried oregano, and crushed red pepper, if using. Then folder the disks in half. Pinch the edges together. Spray the inside of the air fryer basket lightly with olive oil, then place the pizza bites into the basket and cook for 5 to 8 minutes.

Remove and let stand for 3 to 5 minutes before serving.

**PREP TIME:** 10 minutes
**COOK TIME:** 5 to 8 minutes
**TOTAL TIME:** 15 to 18 minutes

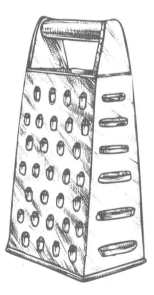

# TOASTED CRUNCHY SUSHI ROLLS

*My first taste of sushi was an eel roll grabbed with girlfriends late one night on a trip to Chicago. I thought I hated all things "of the sea" but decided to be adventurous. Of course, having taste buds, I came to love sushi. Now I love making it with my own unique touches. A handful of cilantro, extra carrots—whatever we're in the mood for. I love using a variety of in-season seafood from TJ's for the meal.*

**FOR THE SUSHI RICE**

2 cups white rice

¼ cup unseasoned rice wine vinegar

¼ cup cane sugar

**FOR THE SRIRACHA MAYO**

1 cup mayonnaise

2 tablespoons sriracha sauce

**FOR THE SUSHI ROLLS**

6 sheets nori

sushi rice

12 to 16 pieces sushi/sashimi-grade fish, crabmeat, shrimp, or other seafood

½ large or 2 small seedless cucumbers, sliced fine

1 cup fresh cilantro, stemmed and chopped

4 green onions, chopped

½ cup panko breadcrumbs

sushi ginger (optional)

soy sauce (optional)

wasabi paste (optional)

**YIELD: 6 SUSHI ROLLS**

### FOR THE SUSHI RICE

Cook rice as directed on the package. (I like to speed things up using my Instant Pot.) When the rice is thoroughly cooked and ready, transfer it to a large bamboo, wooden, glass, or ceramic bowl (avoid metal). Using a wooden or bamboo spoon, stir in the rice wine vinegar and sugar. Mix thoroughly until the rice becomes sticky and aromatic. Let it cool for about 30 minutes or until you can handle it comfortably.

### FOR THE SRIRACHA MAYO

In a shallow bowl, combine the mayonnaise and sriracha and blend thoroughly. Set aside.

### FOR THE SUSHI ROLLS

Preheat the air fryer to 390°F. Once the sushi rice is cool, lay out the nori on your sushi rolling mat or on a tea or kitchen towel layered with plastic wrap (tucked around the ends). Using a spoon or your hands, drop several spoonfuls of sushi rice across the nori, then use the spoon to spread and flatten out the rice as evenly as possible over the nori.

At the end of the nori by the towel or mat's end, create a line of filler. Layer in the fish, the veggies, and the cilantro. Then use the towel or mat to tightly roll the nori around and beyond the filling to completely roll up the sushi.

Now gently coat each sushi roll with sriracha mayo, then roll it in the breadcrumbs. Place the rolls in the air fryer basket and cook at 390°F for 10 minutes.

Remove the sushi rolls from the air fryer and let stand for 2 to 3 minutes. Then slice the rolls into bite-size pieces and serve with sushi ginger, more sriracha mayo, soy sauce, and wasabi paste, if using.

**PREP TIME:** 15 to 20 minutes
**COOK TIME:** 10 minutes
**TOTAL TIME:** 25 to 30 minutes

# CAULIFLOWER GLUTEN-FREE ONION RINGS

*I seriously love onion rings—always have, pretty sure I always will. But, being gluten-free, I just don't get to eat them often. When I discovered the cauliflower baking blend, though, I knew I had to try it in my homemade onion rings recipe. These are some of the tastiest rings I've ever had!*

**1 large white onion, sliced into ¼-inch slices**

**1 cup unsweetened plant-based milk**

**16 ounces Trader Joe's Cassava Cauliflower Blend Baking Mix**

**1 cup gluten-free breadcrumbs**

**1 teaspoon Trader Joe's Everyday Seasoning**

**2 large eggs, lightly beaten**

**olive oil spray**

**YIELD: 6 SERVINGS**

Preheat the air fryer to 390°F. Place the onion slices in a shallow bowl and pour the plant-based milk over them. Cover and let soak for 1 hour in the refrigerator. About 5 minutes before the onions are finished soaking, place the baking mix in a medium mixing bowl. In a separate medium bowl, put the breadcrumbs and seasoning blend. In a third shallow bowl, pour in the beaten eggs.

Remove the onions from the fridge and first, dip them in the flour, dusting off the excess. Then dip them in the eggs, letting the excess drip off. Now coat the rings with breadcrumbs. Lightly spray the inside of the air fryer basket with olive oil spray and lay the onion rings in the basket, side by side, not overlapping.

Cook the onion rings at 390°F for 5 minutes, flip them over with tongs, and cook for another 5 minutes, or until they're crispy. Remove them from the air fryer and let stand 3 to 5 minutes before serving.

**PREP TIME:** 15 minutes
**REST TIME:** 1 hour
**COOK TIME:** 10 minutes
**TOTAL TIME:** 1 hour 25 minutes

# SUPER-EASY, FAST MOZZARELLA STICKS

*Another easy and fast appetizer is this simple mozzarella stick recipe combining two amazing ingredients from Trader Joe's—the mozzarella sticks and the roasted garlic marinara sauce. They make for the perfect movie night snack or party app.*

**olive oil spray**

**1 (16-ounce) package Trader Joe's Breaded Mozzarella Cheese Sticks, frozen**

**½ cup Trader Giotto's Roasted Garlic Marinara Sauce**

**YIELD: 4 SERVINGS**

Preheat your air fryer to 400°F. Lightly spray the air fryer basket with olive oil spray and pour in the mozzarella sticks. Cook for 5 minutes, then shake the basket and cook for another 5 minutes. Remove the sticks from the air fryer and let stand for 2 to 3 minutes before serving with the marinara sauce for dipping.

**PREP TIME:** 2 minutes
**COOK TIME:** 10 minutes
**TOTAL TIME:** 12 minutes

# EASY LEMON-TOMATO TARTS

*Not all tarts have to be sweet. In fact, some of my favorite snacks and light meals are savory tarts like these lemon-tomato tarts. And using TJ's puff pastry makes cooking these so fast and easy.*

1 (18.3-ounce) package Trader Joe's All Butter Puff Pastry

3 tablespoons olive oil, divided

1 teaspoon garlic powder

2 teaspoons dried chives

2 lemons, thinly sliced

3 medium tomatoes, thinly sliced

ground black pepper

pinch of salt

**YIELD: 8 TARTS**

Preheat your air fryer to 375°F. While that's heating up, lay out the puff pastry and cut each sheet into quarters. Prick a few holes into the pastry pieces and set aside. In a small bowl, mix together 2 tablespoons of olive oil, garlic powder, and chives.

Lightly grease 8 ramekins and press the dough squares into each ramekin. Brush the oil and seasoning mixture over the dough, then layer slices of lemon and tomato into each tart. Grind a small amount of black pepper over each tart, along with a pinch of salt. Drizzle the remaining 1 tablespoon of olive oil over the tarts.

Cook the tarts in your air fryer for 15 minutes, or until the edges of the pastry have browned and crisped. Remove the tarts and let them cool for 10 minutes before serving.

**PREP TIME:** 10 minutes
**COOK TIME:** 15 minutes
**TOTAL TIME:** 25 minutes

# Chapter 2

# GIMME SOME SIDES!

# EVERYTHING BUT ELOTE FRIES

*These are a favorite at our house—spicy, slightly cheesy fries. Crisp, zesty, and perfect for dipping in ketchup, BBQ sauce, or just about anything else. They're also great plain, if that's your thing.*

**1 (24-ounce) package Trader Joe's Handsome Cut Potato Fries, frozen**

**olive oil spray**

**1 tablespoon Trader Joe's Everything but the Elote Seasoning Blend**

**YIELD: 8 SERVINGS**

Put the frozen fries in a container with a lid. Gently spray with the olive oil, shaking the fries around to coat them lightly. Sprinkle on seasoning and put the lid on the container. Shake vigorously, making sure the fries are all coated with the seasonings.

Set the air fryer to 400°F. Put the fries in the air fryer basket and cook for 10 minutes. Remove the basket and either shake the fries to resituate them or use tongs to mix them around to move the ones on the bottom to the top. Replace the basket and cook again for another 10 minutes.

Note: if the fries have partially thawed, they'll need only 10 minutes, so you'll want to shake them after 5 minutes.

**PREP TIME:** 3 to 5 minutes
**COOK TIME:** 10 to 20 minutes
**TOTAL TIME:** 13 to 25 minutes

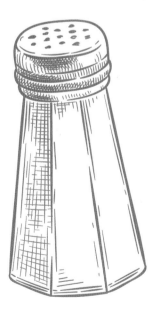

# ROASTED BRUSSELS SPROUTS

*A healthy and delicious side dish is always a great choice—especially when it's this easy. You'll have these savory veggies ready in no time, thanks to your wonderful air fryer.*

**1 (16-ounce) bag Trader Joe's Brussels Sprouts, frozen**

**olive oil spray**

**1½ tablespoons Trader Joe's Spices of the World 21 Seasoning Salute**

**Trader Joe's Spicy Cashew Butter Dressing (optional)**

**YIELD: 5 SERVINGS**

Preheat your air fryer to 350°F for 5 minutes. While that's heating up, empty the bag of brussels sprouts into a plastic container with a lid. Lightly spray the sprouts with olive oil. Put the lid on and gently shake to coat the sprouts. If there's not enough oil to coat them all lightly, add a little more and repeat. Then add the seasoning to the container and shake again to completely coat the sprouts with the seasoning.

When the air fryer is heated up, lightly spray the basket with olive oil and pour in the sprouts. Cook for 10 minutes. Remove the basket and use tongs or a wooden spoon to mix up the sprouts to bring those from the bottom to the top. Return the basket to the air fryer and cook again for 10 minutes.

Let stand for 5 minutes and serve as is or with a light drizzle of the cashew butter dressing, if using.

**PREP TIME:** 3 minutes
**COOK TIME:** 20 minutes
**TOTAL TIME:** 23 minutes

# ZESTY, CRISP TRADER TOTS

*I'm a huge fan of tater tots. Add a little spice and less oil and I'm in heaven! These Trader tots really hit the spot with a pile of sausage and veggies, or as a dinner side with burgers, hot dogs, or so many foods.*

**16 ounces Trader Joe's Trader Potato Tots (approximately ½ package)**

**olive oil spray**

**2 teaspoons Trader Joe's Ajika Georgian Seasoning Blend**

**YIELD: 4 TO 5 SERVINGS**

Lightly spray your air fryer basket with olive oil, then preheat to 350°F for 5 minutes. While the air fryer is heating up, place potato tots in a container with a lid. Lightly spray with olive oil, then sprinkle in the Ajika seasoning. Cover with the lid and shake well to cover the tots with seasoning and oil.

Cook the tots for 5 minutes, shake in the basket, and cook for another 5 minutes. Then let stand for 3 to 5 minutes before serving.

If you like things a little spicier, sprinkle an additional teaspoon of Ajika over the tots in the basket after 5 minutes of cooking, toss gently, and finish cooking.

**PREP TIME:** 2 minutes
**COOK TIME:** 10 minutes
**TOTAL TIME:** 12 minutes

# GARLIC CHEDDAR KNOTS

*Who doesn't love a good cheesy roll? These amazing garlic cheddar knots are amazing and so much faster than the usual "make it yourself" options out there, thanks to Trader Joe's delicious ready-to-bake pizza dough.*

**flour, for rolling**

**16 ounces Trader Giotto's Ready to Bake Garlic & Herb Pizza Dough**

**1 cup shredded cheddar cheese**

**¼ teaspoon ground black pepper**

**2 teaspoons dried oregano**

**2 teaspoons garlic powder**

**olive oil spray**

**YIELD: 8 KNOTS**

Sprinkle flour on a flat, dry, clean surface. Put the dough on the surface, spreading it out and kneading it with your hands. Sprinkle cheese and seasonings evenly over the dough. Fold dough in on itself and knead together, blending the ingredients. Break dough into 8 even pieces. In your hands, roll each piece into a ball, then roll out into a thick rope. Fold each rope in half and gently pinch together to keep shape.

Preheat your air fryer to 400°F. Spray lightly with olive oil, then place the knots in the basket, not overlapping. Spray knots with more olive oil. Cook for 3 to 5 minutes. Remove them and let stand for 5 minutes before serving.

**PREP TIME:** 5 to 7 minutes
**COOK TIME:** 3 to 5 minutes
**TOTAL TIME:** 8 to 12 minutes

# SWEET POTATO FRITES

*For a quick, easy, and delicious side that works with burgers, hot dogs, or practically anything else in the American cuisine realm, whip these up.*

olive oil spray

1 (15-ounce) bag Trader Joe's Sweet Potato Frites, frozen

½ teaspoon dried cilantro

1 teaspoon dried chives

2 teaspoons Italian seasoning

½ teaspoon dried rosemary

½ teaspoon dried thyme leaves

1 teaspoon Trader Joe's Everything but the Bagel Seasoning Blend

**YIELD: 5 SERVINGS**

Preheat the air fryer to 350°F for 5 minutes. Lightly spray the inside of the basket with olive oil. In a container with a lid, add the frites. Spray lightly with oil, then add the seasonings. Cover and shake vigorously to coat the frites. Cook for 10 minutes, then shake the basket to expose the buried frites. Cook for another 10 minutes. Let stand for 3 minutes, then serve.

**PREP TIME:** 5 minutes
**COOK TIME:** 20 minutes
**TOTAL TIME:** 25 minutes

# CHEESY ELOTE SWEET POTATO FRITES

*In our house, cheese is the magic word. If you're not sure something will taste good, add cheese. If you know something will taste good—it can be improved with cheese. Sweet potato frites are no exception. And the Everything But the Elote Seasoning Blend just sends these over the top in goodness.*

**1 (15-ounce) bag Trader Joe's Sweet Potato Frites, frozen**

**olive oil spray**

**2 teaspoons Trader Joe's Everything but the Elote Seasoning Blend**

**¾ cup shredded cheddar cheese**

**YIELD: 5 SERVINGS**

Preheat the air fryer to 350°F for 5 minutes. Spray the inside of the basket. Dump the bag of frites into a container with a lid. Spray the frites lightly with olive oil, then add in the seasoning. Cover and shake vigorously to coat the frites. Add it to the basket and cook for 10 minutes. Shake the basket to expose the frites from the bottom and cook for another 10 minutes. Sprinkle the cheddar over the frites and cook for another 3 minutes. Let stand for 3 minutes, and serve.

**PREP TIME:** 5 minutes
**COOK TIME:** 23 minutes
**TOTAL TIME:** 28 minutes

Gimme Some Sides!

# CARNE ASADA NACHO FRITES

*If you've never had loaded nacho fries, you are missing out! These tasty treats are super easy to make and can easily be used as either a side or a full meal—whichever suits you best.*

1½ pounds Trader Joe's Carne Asada Autentica beef

olive oil spray

1 (24-ounce) package Trader Joe's Handsome Cut Potato Fries, frozen

1 cup cheddar cheese sauce or nacho sauce

¼ cup sour cream

½ cup Trader Joe's Mild Pico de Gallo Salsa

4 green onions, chopped

handful of banana pepper slices (optional)

½ cup Trader Joe's Chunky Guacamole

**YIELD: 4 TO 6 SERVINGS**

Preheat the air fryer to 375°F. Place the carne asada into a medium air-fryer pan and cook for 10 minutes. Flip over the meat and cook for another 10 minutes. Remove the meat and set aside. Lightly spray with olive oil the air fryer basket, then place the fries in the air fryer basket and cook for 15 minutes, shaking the basket every 5 minutes.

Remove the fries from the basket and plate them. Next, add cheddar cheese sauce (or nacho sauce, if using) to the fries. Cut the carne asada into bite-size chunks and layer on the fries, then top with sour cream, pico de gallo, green onions, and banana pepper slices, if using, then garnish with guacamole.

**PREP TIME:** 10 minutes
**COOK TIME:** 35 minutes
**TOTAL TIME:** 45 minutes

# LOADED TRADER TOTS

*In case you couldn't tell by all my tots recipes, I adore TJ's tots (and, well, let's be honest, all tots). So, here's another take on how to best use them for a fun side dish the whole family can enjoy—especially the BBQ lovers among you.*

olive oil spray

**1 pound Trader Joe's Trader Potato Tots, frozen (approximately ½ package)**

**1 pound ground turkey or bacon, cooked and drained**

**2 jalapeños, seeded and chopped fine**

**1 (14.5-ounce) can diced tomatoes**

**2 teaspoons Trader Joe's Cuban Style Citrusy Garlic Seasoning Blend**

**½ cup Trader Joe's Carolina Gold Barbeque Sauce**

**¼ cup sour cream**

**1 cup shredded cheddar cheese**

**YIELD: 6 TO 8 SERVINGS**

Preheat the air fryer to 400°F for 5 minutes. Lightly spray the basket with olive oil, then put the potato tots in. Cook for 5 minutes. Shake the basket and cook for another 5 minutes. While they're cooking, combine in a medium bowl the ground turkey or bacon, jalapeños, diced tomatoes, and seasoning. Mix together thoroughly.

Remove the potato tots and put them in the air fryer pan. Layer on the meat mixture, then drizzle the barbecue sauce and sour cream over them. Now top with cheese. Reduce heat to 350°F and cook the tot mix for 3 minutes, until the cheese melts slightly. Serve immediately.

**PREP TIME:** 7 minutes
**COOK TIME:** 13 minutes
**TOTAL TIME:** 20 minutes

# LOADED POTATO CHIPS

*I'm all about loaded everything, in case you haven't figured that out. Technically, these are all sides, but I personally love making these for meals. They're filling enough and taste amazing, so I'm good to go.*

2 large russet potatoes

olive oil spray

4 teaspoons Trader Joe's Chile Lime Seasoning Blend, divided

½ cup shredded cheddar cheese

¼ cup whipped cream cheese

¼ cup Trader Joe's Soy Chorizo, cooked and crumbled

**YIELD: 4 SERVINGS**

Wash and slice the potatoes into pieces about 1/8 inch thick. Place the potato slices in paper towels to soak up the liquid for 10 minutes. Preheat the air fryer to 400°F. Put the potato slices in a bag or container that fits them and that seals. Lightly spray olive oil over the potatoes, then sprinkle in 2 teaspoons of the seasoning. Cover and shake vigorously until the potatoes are fully coated.

Put the potato slices in the air fryer basket and cook for 10 minutes. Toss the chips and cook for an additional 5 minutes. If you want the chips a little crisper, cook for another 5 minutes. Remove the chips from the air fryer and place on a large serving platter.

Immediately sprinkle the cheddar cheese over the chips and let the cheese melt slightly for 2 to 3 minutes. Sprinkle the remaining 2 teaspoons of seasoning into the whipped cream cheese and mix until thoroughly combined. Then layer on the whipped cream cheese and cooked chorizo. Serve immediately.

**PREP TIME:** 20 minutes
**REST TIME:** 10 minutes
**COOK TIME:** 17 to 23 minutes
**TOTAL TIME:** 47 to 53 minutes

# CITRUSY GARLIC PARMESAN MUSHROOMS

*Here's an easy side that kind of feels fancy (to me at least!). These little shrooms pair perfectly with steak, burgers, sandwiches, even salads.*

**1 pound white mushrooms, washed and stemmed**

**2 tablespoons olive oil**

**2 teaspoons Trader Joe's Cuban Style Citrusy Garlic Seasoning Blend**

**olive oil spray**

**¼ cup shredded parmesan cheese**

**YIELD: 4 TO 6 SERVINGS**

Preheat your air fryer to 370°F. While that's heating up, toss the mushrooms into a container with a lid. Pour in the olive oil and seasoning. Cover the container and shake vigorously, coating the mushrooms completely. Spray the air fryer basket with olive oil spray, then place the mushrooms in the basket. Cook for 7 minutes, then shake the basket. Cook for an additional 7 minutes. Sprinkle in the parmesan cheese and cook for another 3 minutes, or until the cheese melts. Remove the shrooms from the air fryer and let stand 2 to 3 minutes before serving.

**PREP TIME:** 3 minutes
**COOK TIME:** 17 minutes
**TOTAL TIME:** 20 minutes

# STUFFED MUSHROOMS

*These stuffed mushrooms are inspired by Trader Joe's new Green Goddess Gouda. The savory, herby flavors are perfect for mushrooms in the air fryer. Definitely a new holiday favorite in our household.*

4 ounces Trader Joe's Green Goddess Gouda, crumbled or chopped fine

4 ounces cream cheese

2 to 3 strips bacon, cooked and crumbled

1 teaspoon Trader Joe's South African Smoke Seasoning Blend

olive oil spray

12 cremini mushrooms (also known as baby portabellas), washed and stemmed

**YIELD: 4 SERVINGS**

In a small mixing bowl, combine the gouda, cream cheese, bacon crumbles, and seasoning blend. Preheat the air fryer to 360°F. Lightly spray the air fryer basket with olive oil. Stuff the cheese mix into the mushroom caps and carefully place them in the air fryer basket, stuffing side up. Cook for 8 minutes. Cheese should be melted and slightly browned. Cook for an additional 2 to 3 minutes if not browned enough for your taste. Remove from the air fryer with small tongs and let stand for 3 minutes before serving.

**PREP TIME:** 7 minutes
**COOK TIME:** 8 to 11 minutes
**TOTAL TIME:** 15 to 18 minutes

# Chapter 3

# PRODUCE THE SNACKS!

# ACAI OAT PROTEIN BALLS

*Notwithstanding some of the recipes in here (I'm looking at you, Fig Bars!), I'm actually all about healthy options for keeping life light, energetic, and delicious. When I discovered TJ's Pea Protein Powder, I realized I'd found the perfect healthy protein powder to bake with. So, for my energy balls, this stuff is now my go-to. And for some flavor and added energy, the acai puree and wild blueberries make the day.*

**1 cup Trader Joe's Organic Pea Protein Powder**

**2 cups old fashioned oats**

**pinch of salt**

**4 tablespoons Trader Joe's Raw & Unfiltered Hawaiian Macadamia Nut Blossom & Multi-Floral Honey**

**2 (3.52-ounce) packets of Trader Joe's Unsweetened Organic Acai Puree, thawed**

**1 tablespoon vanilla extract**

**¼ cup water**

**1 cup frozen wild blueberries, thawed**

**YIELD: 35 TO 40 ENERGY BALLS**

In a medium mixing bowl, whisk together the pea protein powder, old fashioned oats, and salt. Add in the honey, followed by the acai puree, vanilla, and water. Mix together thoroughly, then toss in the blueberries and mix together one last time.

Preheat the air fryer to 375°F for 5 minutes. While that's heating up, grab approximately 1 tablespoon of the mix in your hands and roll into a ball. Place the ball on parchment paper on a pan for the air fryer. Repeat with all the mix until the full amount is in the balls. Place the pan in the air fryer and cook for 3 to 4 minutes.

Remove the balls from the air fryer and let cool completely before snacking on them.

**PREP TIME:** 10 minutes
**COOK TIME:** 3 to 4 minutes
**TOTAL TIME:** 13 to 14 minutes

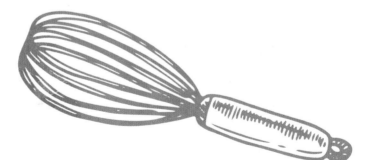

# CHEWY CHOCOLATE PROTEIN CHERRY BOMBS

*Another reasonably healthy energy protein treat comes in the form of these sweet, chocolatey cherry bombs. They're decadent, for sure, and chewy, but they pack a punch of energy and don't use a ton of sugar.*

**2 cups Trader Joe's Pitted Dark Sweet Cherries, frozen**

**2 tablespoons almond flour**

**1 cup oat flour**

**2 tablespoons pure cocoa powder**

**¼ cup Trader Joe's Organic Pea Protein Powder**

**¼ cup cane sugar**

**½ cup sweetened vanilla almond milk**

**1 tablespoon vanilla extract**

**2 tablespoons water**

**YIELD: 10 TO 12 TREATS**

Set out the cherries to start thawing while you work. Preheat the air fryer to 375°F for 5 minutes. In a medium mixing bowl, whisk together all the dry ingredients. Add in the almond milk, vanilla extract, and water and blend together. Finally, mix in the cherries with a wooden spoon. If the mix seems a little dry, add in another tablespoon of water.

Spoon out approximately three cherries and a tablespoon of the batter onto parchment paper on a baking sheet. Repeat until the bowl is empty, keeping the bombs separated on the parchment paper. Cook the cherry bombs for 5 minutes. They should be solid but a bit spongy when you remove them from the air fryer. Let cool completely before serving.

**PREP TIME:** 5 minutes
**COOK TIME:** 5 minutes
**TOTAL TIME:** 10 minutes

# EVERYTHING FRIED PICKLES

*Growing up in the South, I've eaten a lot of fried pickles. And they've been good. But there's just something about that Everything but the Bagel seasoning that really sends these over the top.*

**32 dill pickle slices**

**½ cup all-purpose flour**

**2 teaspoon Trader Joe's Everything but the Bagel Seasoning Blend**

**3 large eggs, beaten**

**¼ cup pickle juice**

**2 cups panko breadcrumbs**

**2 tablespoons fresh dill, snipped**

**olive oil spray**

**Trader Joe's Organic Ranch Dressing, for dipping (optional)**

**YIELD: 32 SLICES**

Place the pickle slices on paper towels to drain for about 15 minutes. Preheat your air fryer to 400°F. While that's going on, combine the flour and seasoning blend in a shallow bowl. In a separate medium bowl, whisk together the eggs and pickle juice. In a third separate shallow bowl, combine the panko and fresh dill.

Dip the pickles into the flour mixture, coating on both sides. Shake off the excess. Then dip them into the egg mixture, patting them off to help the coating stick. Then dip into the panko mixture. Gently coat the air fryer basket with olive oil spray and set the pickles in the air fryer, not overlapping. Cook for 7 to 10 minutes, until crispy. Turn the pickles over and spritz with some olive oil, then cook for another 7 minutes. Repeat with the remainder of the pickle slices until all are cooked.

Serve immediately with ranch dressing, if using.

**PREP TIME:** 10 minutes
**COOK TIME:** 14 to 17 minutes
**TOTAL TIME:** 24 to 30 minutes

# BUFFALO TRADER TOTS

*I've personally never been big into Buffalo wings but, man, they sure have smelled good lately when I've whipped some up for my hubby. Since I can't eat glutinous wings, I thought, why not tots? So, I made these up and now we enjoy a nice gluten-free treat for movie nights.*

**olive oil spray**

**½ (32-ounce) bag Trader Joe's Trader Potato Tots**

**3 tablespoons Buffalo wing sauce**

**Trader Joe's Crumbled Blue Cheese or Trader Joe's Chunky Blue Cheese Dressing & Dip (optional)**

**YIELD: 8 SERVINGS**

Preheat the air fryer to 390°F for 5 minutes. Lightly spray the basket with olive oil, then add the potato tots. Cook for 20 minutes, shaking once or twice. Remove the tots and put them in an air fryer pan and add the Buffalo sauce. Toss together until the tots are coated. Put the pan in the air fryer and cook for another 5 minutes.

Remove the tots from the air fryer and plate, adding blue cheese crumbles or dressing on the side, if using. Serve immediately.

**PREP TIME:** 5 minutes
**COOK TIME:** 25 minutes
**TOTAL TIME:** 30 minutes

# MAC AND CHEESE BITES

*Here's another super-easy one for us rush-around types. They're fast, tasty, delicious, and kind of fun for everyone. I like to produce them for the hubby when I'm on my way out to social events and he just needs a little extra "something" while I'm gone.*

**1 (10-ounce) package Trader Joe's Mac and Cheese Bites**

**olive oil spray**

**Trader Joe's Organic Sriracha and Roasted Garlic BBQ Sauce**

**YIELD: 10 BITES (APPROXIMATELY 3 SERVINGS)**

Preheat your air fryer to 360°F. Lightly spray the basket with olive oil spray, then line the basket with the mac and cheese bites, not overlapping. Cook for 4 to 5 minutes. Using tongs, flip the bites over and cook for another 4 to 5 minutes, or until they turn golden-brown. They should be soft to the touch. Remove them from the air fryer and serve with the BBQ sauce. Alternatively, you could use marinara or Alfredo sauces, or even Trader Joe's Honey Aleppo Sauce for dipping.

**PREP TIME:** 5 minutes
**COOK TIME:** 8 to 10 minutes
**TOTAL TIME:** 13 to 15 minutes

# EVERYTHING BUT THE BAGEL PUFF PASTRY CHEDDAR STRAWS

*For those looking for an easy, tasty, cheesy, bready type of snack, these cheese straws are perfect. The puff pastry makes them light and fluffy, while the cheese and seasoning send the flavor over the top.*

**1 (18.3-ounce) package Trader Joe's All Butter Puff Pastry**

**½ cup grated parmesan cheese**

**3 tablespoons Trader Joe's Everything but the Bagel Seasoning Blend**

**YIELD: 18 STRAWS**

Roll out the puff pastry on a lightly floured flat surface. Sprinkle about half the parmesan and half the seasoning blend over the sheets of puff pastry. Gently press the cheese and spices into the dough, then flip the dough over and repeat the process with the remaining cheese and spices.

Cut each sheet into roughly 1-inch strips. Then twist each strip by holding both ends and twisting them in opposite directions. Place the straws in the fridge and chill for about 1 hour.

Preheat your air fryer to 400°F. Remove the straws from the fridge and place them on parchment paper in the air fryer basket, not overlapping. Cook for 10 minutes, or until puffed and crispy. Remove them from the air fryer and let stand for about 5 minutes before serving.

**PREP TIME:** 10 minutes
**COOK TIME:** 10 minutes
**TOTAL TIME:** 20 minutes

# PIGS IN A PUFFY BLANKET

*Pigs in a blanket is always another favorite treat. Personally, I love the light, fluffy texture of puff pastry and so does my husband. For an extra special treat, I've combined the two concepts, along with some amazing seasoning, to make these pigs in a puffy blanket.*

**1 (18.3-ounce) package Trader Joe's All Butter Puff Pastry**

**4 teaspoons Trader Joe's Everything but the Bagel Seasoning Blend**

**1 (12-ounce) package Trader Joe's Cocktail Pups**

**olive oil spray**

**YIELD: 16 PIECES**

Lay out the puff pastry sheets on a wax paper–lined baking sheet. Lightly sprinkle 1 teaspoon of seasoning mix on each sheet. Flip the sheets over and sprinkle with the remaining 2 teaspoons seasoning. Then use a butter knife to cut the sheets into 8 squares per sheet.

Set the air fryer to 325°F and preheat for 5 minutes. While the air fryer is heating up, place a cocktail pup in each of the squares and fold two corners up around the pup. Pinch together.

Spray the air fryer basket with olive oil, then place the wrapped cocktail pups in the air fryer basket, not overlapping. Cook for 3 to 4 minutes or until the pastry turns golden-brown. Let stand for 5 minutes, then serve.

**PREP TIME:** 5 to 7 minutes
**COOK TIME:** 3 to 4 minutes
**TOTAL TIME:** 8 to 11 minutes

# PLANTAIN CHIPS

*I love grabbing fresh produce from TJ's and turning it into delicious homemade treats. And having fallen for plantain chips while I lived in Guatemala, there's something extra special about making these deliciously crispy treats at home.*

**2 plantains**

**4 teaspoons garlic powder, divided**

**2 cups water**

**2 tablespoons coconut oil**

**1 teaspoon fresh chives, snipped**

**1 teaspoon onion powder**

**coconut oil spray**

**YIELD: 4 SERVINGS**

Peel the plantains by cutting 2 or 3 slits through the skin, then peeling with a knife or peeler. In a small bowl, mix 2 teaspoons of garlic powder with the water. Place the peeled plantains in the water and soak for 30 minutes. Once they've soaked, remove them from the water and pat dry with a kitchen towel.

Slice the plantains thinly with a knife or mandoline, then put the slices in a container with a lid. Pour in the liquid coconut oil, the rest of the garlic powder, the chives, and the onion powder. Cover and toss until the chips are thoroughly coated.

Preheat the air fryer to 350°F. Lightly spray some coconut oil spray in the air fryer basket, then put the chips in the basket. Cook for 5 minutes, toss, and cook again for 5 minutes. Toss the basket again and cook for another 5 to 7 minutes until the chips are slightly browned and crispy. Remove the chips and spread them out on a tea towel to drain and dry completely before serving.

**PREP TIME:** 12 minutes
**REST TIME:** 30 minutes
**COOK TIME:** 15 to 17 minutes
**TOTAL TIME:** 57 to 59 minutes

# PUFF PASTRY CREAM CHEESE AND SAUSAGE TARTS

*Another easy, fun snack is these puff-pastry meat and cheese tarts. They're absolutely delicious—almost decadent—and don't take much time or energy to make.*

**8 ounces cream cheese, softened**

**3 links Trader Joe's Sweet Apple Chicken Sausage, diced**

**1 (18.3-ounce) package Trader Joe's All Butter Puff Pastry**

**1 large egg, lightly beaten**

**fresh cilantro, for garnish (optional)**

**YIELD: 4 LARGE TARTS**

Preheat the air fryer to 400°F. In a medium mixing bowl, blend the cream cheese and sausage together with a fork. Set aside. Place the puff pastry dough on a parchment paper-lined baking sheet and baste one sheet with egg. Then cut each sheet into quarters and place 1 unbasted square into each of 4 lightly greased ramekins, pressing the dough into the bottom and sides. Fill each dough cup with the cheese and sausage mixture, then gently press the egg-basted pastry squares over the ramekins to create the tart tops.

Cook the tarts in the air fryer for 10 to 12 minutes, or until the crust is golden-brown. Remove from the air fryer and let stand for 10 minutes before serving. If desired, garnish with fresh cilantro.

**PREP TIME:** 10 minutes
**COOK TIME:** 10 to 12 minutes
**TOTAL TIME:** 20 to 22 minutes

# EASY CHEESY SPINACH PUFFS

*There's something about feta and spinach together. The combo is amazing on pizza, in sauces, on salads. But mix them with seasonings inside puff pastry and you've got something even more stellar.*

**4 cups fresh spinach, completely dry, chopped**

**½ cup Trader Joe's Crumbled Feta**

**¼ white onion, minced**

**1 tablespoon olive oil**

**1 teaspoon garlic powder**

**¼ teaspoon ground black pepper**

**2 large eggs, lightly beaten separately**

**1 (18.3-ounce) package Trader Joe's All Butter Puff Pastry**

**YIELD: 8 PUFFS**

Mix the spinach, feta, onion, olive oil, garlic powder, and black pepper in a medium bowl. Then beat in 1 egg. Set aside.

Preheat the air fryer to 400°F. Lay out the pastry dough on a flat, dry surface. Cut each sheet of the dough into quarters, baste with the other egg, then place into muffin cups or silicone muffin wrappers. Fill each cup with the spinach mixture, then pull the corners over the filling and pinch together in the center. Place the muffin cups in the air fryer and cook for 7 to 10 minutes, or until the pastry turns golden-brown. Let stand 5 minutes before serving.

**PREP TIME:** 10 minutes
**COOK TIME:** 7 to 10 minutes
**TOTAL TIME:** 17 to 20 minutes

# HOT 'N SPICY HARISSA ALMOND BITES

*These are a spicy treat for folks who love something a little different. And when I say spicy, I mean hot. The harissa is a traditional hot pepper/tomato paste that should be used in very small amounts, unless you're looking for a fire in your mouth.*

**16 ounces Trader Giotto's Ready to Bake Garlic & Herb Pizza Dough**

**flour, for rolling**

**Trader Joe's Traditional Tunisian Harissa paste**

**several pieces Trader Joe's Mushroom Medley**

**several pieces Trader Joe's Nuts Raw Sliced Almonds**

**olive oil spray**

**YIELD: 20 TO 24 BITES**

Split the dough into two pieces and set aside. Sprinkle flour on a flat, clean, dry surface. Take one piece of the dough and roll it out to about ¼-inch thick. Use a cup or round biscuit cutter to make circles about 4 inches in diameter.

Now spread ¼ teaspoon of harissa paste in the center of each circle. Be sure to use very little unless you want a hot surprise on the other side! It's very spicy. Next, add 3 to 4 small mushroom medley pieces, and 4 to 6 almond slices. Then fold up together into the center, pinching together.

Preheat the air fryer to 400°F. Spray the interior of your air fryer basket with olive oil. Place the harissa bites in the basket and gently spray them. Cook for 5 minutes. Remove them and let stand for 2 minutes before serving.

**PREP TIME:** 10 to 15 minutes
**COOK TIME:** 5 minutes
**TOTAL TIME:** 15 to 20 minutes

# Chapter 4

# DID SOMEBODY SAY SALAD?

# TWISTED BROCCOLI SLAW

*For a twist on the typical slaw, this broccoli slaw is roasted and uses a nontraditional dressing for a spicy taste that even those not terribly fond of broccoli are bound to love.*

**1 (12-ounce) package Trader Joe's Organic Broccoli Slaw**

**olive oil spray**

**1 tablespoon za'atar seasoning**

**2 tablespoons roasted, salted sunflower seeds**

**4 tablespoons raisins**

**6 tablespoons Trader Joe's Spicy Cashew Butter Dressing**

**YIELD: 4 TO 6 SERVINGS**

Preheat your air fryer to 350°F for 5 minutes. While that's heating up, dump the slaw into a plastic container with a lid. Lightly spray with olive oil and sprinkle the za'atar seasoning over it. Put the lid on and shake vigorously, coating everything as evenly as possible.

When the air fryer is ready, dump the slaw into the basket and cook for 5 minutes. Take the basket out, shake the slaw around a bit, then cook again for another 5 minutes.

Let the slaw stand for 5 minutes, then return it to the plastic container. Add in the sunflower seeds, raisins, and dressing. Chill for an hour, then serve.

**PREP TIME:** 3 to 5 minutes
**COOK TIME:** 10 minutes
**TOTAL TIME:** 13 to 15 minutes

# TURKEY MEATBALL MEDLEY SALAD

*This one has just the perfect amount of "spicy" in it to really bring out the yum in some otherwise basic ingredients. The turkey meatballs, of course, are tasty as is, and who doesn't love Trader Joe's carrot coins? But tossing in just a hint of seasoning and spicing it up with this amazing dressing brings it all together.*

olive oil spray

1 (16-ounce) package Trader Joe's Turkey Meatballs, frozen

1 (14-ounce) package Trader Joe's Colorful Carrot Coins, frozen

1 tablespoon Trader Joe's Spices of the World 21 Seasoning Salute

1 heart of romaine

Trader Joe's Spicy Cashew Butter Dressing

**YIELD: 6 SERVINGS**

Spray the inside of your air fryer basket with olive oil spray, then preheat to 400°F for 5 minutes. Place the meatballs in the air fryer basket and cook for 10 minutes.

While the meatballs are cooking, dump the carrot coins into a plastic container with a lid. Lightly spray the coins with olive oil and sprinkle 1 tablespoon of 21 Seasoning Salute blend over them. Put the lid on and shake gently, coating the coins with oil and seasoning.

Add the carrot coins to the meatballs in the air fryer basket and shake or stir them together. Cook for another 10 minutes, then remove them. While they're cooling, cut up your romaine and plate it. Top the lettuce with the meatball/coin medley and top that with the dressing.

**PREP TIME:** 3 to 5 minutes
**COOK TIME:** 20 minutes
**TOTAL TIME:** 23 to 25 minutes

# CRISPY ASIAN TOFU SALAD

*In our house, we love everything Asian inspired. And salads are no exception! When I spotted the baked teriyaki tofu at TJ's, I immediately envisioned this exact salad. My husband's not a huge fan of tofu, but he was still begging for more of this delicious meal.*

1 (7-ounce) package Trader Joe's Organic Baked Tofu Terikayi Flavor

1 large romaine heart

½ large red onion

2 teaspoons sesame seeds

2 tablespoons unsalted, roasted peanuts

Trader Joe's Asian Style Spicy Peanut Vinaigrette

**YIELD: 2 SERVINGS**

Cut the tofu into cubes and lay them in your air fryer basket. Make sure none of the pieces are overlapping. Cook the tofu for 5 minutes, then turn over with tongs and cook for another 5 minutes.

While the tofu is cooking, chop up your romaine and onion into bite-size pieces, and plate the romaine. Remove the tofu from the basket and divvy it up among the plates of romaine. Top with the red onion, sprinkle with 1 teaspoon sesame seeds and 1 tablespoon peanuts per salad, and top with the Asian-style dressing. Serve immediately for the tastiest results.

**PREP TIME:** 2 minutes
**COOK TIME:** 10 minutes
**TOTAL TIME:** 12 minutes

# EASY CHORIZO SALAD

*This super-simple recipe is astonishingly delicious. And super quick and easy to make—so, yeah. Can't beat it!*

**6 ounces Trader Joe's Soy Chorizo**

**2 romaine hearts**

**1 cup shredded cheddar cheese**

**4 servings Trader Joe's Sun-Dried Tomatoes**

**Trader Joe's Spicy Cashew Butter Dressing**

**YIELD: 4 SALADS**

Lightly spray the air fryer basket and preheat the air fryer to 350°F for 5 minutes. Prick tiny holes in the chorizo and place in the basket. Cook for 7 to 9 minutes.

While the chorizo is cooking, chop up your romaine and plate. Sprinkle the cheddar cheese over the lettuce. When the chorizo is ready, cut the casing open and spoon out the chorizo over the salad. Add the sun-dried tomatoes and top with the dressing. Serve immediately.

**PREP TIME:** 5 minutes
**COOK TIME:** 7 to 9 minutes
**TOTAL TIME:** 12 to 14 minutes

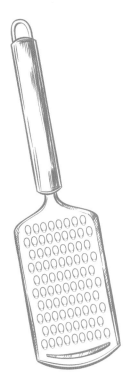

# GYRO SALAD

*This is a super-easy way to treat the family to something special without having to spend a long time over a hot stove. And it all starts with Trader Joe's amazing gyro slices. Easy, fast, delicious.*

1 (8-ounce) package Trader Joe's Gyro Slices

2 hearts of romaine

2 Roma tomatoes

½ white onion, sliced

¼ cup Trader Joe's Marinated Olive Duo with Lemon and Herbs

6 to 8 tablespoons Trader Joe's Greek Style Feta Dressing

**YIELD: 4 SERVINGS**

Lay out the gyro slices in the air fryer basket and cook for 7 minutes at 375°F. Remove from the basket and place them on a plate with paper towels to help remove grease. Meat should be crisp. Pat off excess grease with additional paper towels and let cool.

Chop up the romaine hearts and Roma tomatoes and toss together in a large bowl with white onion and olives. When the meat has cooled, break it into chunks and spread across the salad. Top with feta dressing and mix together thoroughly before serving.

**PREP TIME:** 5 minutes
**COOK TIME:** 7 minutes
**TOTAL TIME:** 12 minutes

# CHICKEN SHAWARMA SALAD

*Trying new kinds of salad is one of my joys in life. Add in Trader Joe's ingredients and I'm about as happy as I can be—foodwise, at least! And I'm a huge fan of all things Mediterranean, so this delicious salad really does it for me.*

**2 pounds Trader Joe's Shawarma Chicken Thighs**

**2 heads of romaine lettuce**

**2 large tomatoes**

**1 white onion**

**Trader Joe's Tzatziki Creamy Garlic Cucumber Dip**

**YIELD: 6 SERVINGS**

Preheat the air fryer to 400°F for 5 minutes. Place the chicken and all the saucy goodness from the package into a medium air fryer pan and cook for 15 minutes. Stir the chicken, exposing the undercooked chicken and bringing it to the top of the pan. Cook for another 15 minutes.

While the chicken is cooking for the second round, chop your lettuce, tomatoes, and onions for the salad and plate the onion and lettuce.

When the chicken is done cooking, remove it from the air fryer. Top with tomatoes and let stand for 3 to 5 minutes. Cut the chicken into equal portions and place it over the salad. Top with a healthy dollop of the tzatziki dip and enjoy!

**PREP TIME:** 7 to 10 minutes
**COOK TIME:** 30 minutes
**TOTAL TIME:** 37 to 40 minutes

# TOASTED CURRY GARBANZO QUINOA SALAD

*I love this salad! I used to think curry was only for soups and meats, but then, odd as it sounds, I tried a peanut butter curry ice cream from a specialty shop in Guatemala. Trying that amazingly unique sweet treat opened up the world for me on how to use curry differently. I highly encourage you to make this salad to start your own curry journey and get creative with the spice.*

**1 (15-ounce) can Trader Joe's Organic Garbanzo Beans**

**2 tablespoons red wine vinegar**

**2 teaspoons olive oil**

**2 teaspoons curry powder**

**½ teaspoon ground turmeric**

**½ teaspoon ground coriander seed**

**1 teaspoon ground cumin**

**1 tablespoon Trader Joe's Honey Aleppo Sauce, more for topping**

**4 cups arugula**

**2 cups tricolor quinoa, cooked**

**YIELD: 4 SERVINGS**

In a container with a lid, combine the garbanzos, vinegar, oil, seasonings, and Aleppo sauce. Cover and gently shake to coat the garbanzos completely. Put the garbanzos in the air fryer basket and cook at 400°F for 15 minutes, shaking every 5 minutes.

While that's cooking, plate the arugula, topped with the quinoa, evenly across 4 plates. Remove the garbanzos from the air fryer and top the salads. Drizzle a little more Aleppo sauce over the salads, as desired. Serve.

**PREP TIME:** 10 minutes
**COOK TIME:** 15 minutes
**TOTAL TIME:** 25 minutes

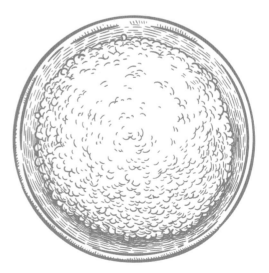

# BUFFALO CHICKEN SALAD

*My hubby adores anything Buffalo, so creating an easy air fryer Buffalo chicken salad made sense to me. The results are pretty delicious, so I wasn't wrong.*

**2 boneless, skinless chicken breasts**

**¼ cup Buffalo wing sauce**

**8 cups chopped romaine**

**1 stalk celery, chopped**

**2 carrots, peeled and shredded**

**1 cup cherry tomatoes**

**½ cup Trader Joe's Chunky Blue Cheese Dressing & Dip**

**YIELD: 4 SERVINGS**

Put the chicken and Buffalo sauce into a sealable container. Shake vigorously, coating the chicken well. Put in the fridge and let chill for 1 hour. Preheat the air fryer to 375°F. Remove the chicken from the container and place directly in the air fryer basket. Cook for 15 minutes, flip the chicken, and cook for another 10 minutes or until internal temperature reaches 165°F.

Put the romaine, celery, carrots and tomatoes into a large bowl and toss together. Plate the salad on 4 plates. Slice the chicken and evenly distribute across the plates. Drizzle the dressing over the salads, and serve.

**PREP TIME:** 10 minutes
**REST TIME:** 1 hour
**COOK TIME:** 25 minutes
**TOTAL TIME:** 1 hour 35 minutes

# AIR FRYER SOUTHWESTERN SALAD

*A fast, easy, veggie-heavy salad is always a win in my book. This delightful Southwestern option makes for great lunches at work, school, and home.*

1 (15-ounce) can Trader Joe's Organic Garbanzo Beans

1 jalapeño, seeded and chopped fine

1 red bell pepper, chopped

½ small red onion, sliced thin

1 cup frozen corn kernels

2 tablespoons olive oil

1 tablespoon taco seasoning

1 teaspoon ground mustard

2 hearts romaine, chopped

½ cucumber, chopped

¼ cup Trader Joe's Spicy Cashew Butter Dressing

**YIELD: 4 SERVINGS**

Preheat the air fryer to 350°F. While that's heating, drain and rinse the garbanzo beans, then toss together with the jalapeño, bell pepper, onion, and corn in a container with a lid. Pour in the olive oil, then add the taco seasoning and mustard. Seal the container and shake to thoroughly coat the garbanzos and veggies. Put the mix in the air fryer basket and cook for 10 minutes, shaking once in the middle. Remove the blend and put into a bowl with the cucumber and romaine. Drizzle dressing over, and serve.

**PREP TIME:** 10 minutes
**COOK TIME:** 10 minutes
**TOTAL TIME:** 20 minutes

# AIR FRYER SOFFRITTO CAPRESE SALAD

*I love a little spiciness in my salads, so this soffritto caprese salad is a special treat on wintry days when a little zing can really boost the mood.*

**1 cup cherry tomatoes**

**2 cloves garlic, minced**

**½ teaspoon Trader Joe's Italian Style Soffritto Seasoning Blend**

**¼ cup Trader Joe's Organic Balsamic & Fig Dressing, divided**

**2 romaine hearts, cut in half lengthwise**

**Half container Trader Joe's Burrata cheese (approximately 4 ounces), drained**

**YIELD: 2 LARGE SALADS**

Preheat the air fryer to 400°F. While that's heating up, place the tomatoes, garlic, seasoning blend, and half the dressing into a bowl. Gently toss together, coating everything with the dressing. Place the tomatoes in the air fryer basket and cook for 3 minutes. Shake the basket and cook for another 3 minutes. Remove the tomatoes and set aside.

Place romaine hearts in the air fryer basket, cut side down, and cook for 3 minutes. Flip the hearts and cook for an additional 2 minutes. Remove and plate the lettuce. Top with the tomatoes and the burrata, and then drizzle the remaining dressing over the salad. Serve immediately.

**PREP TIME:** 10 minutes
**COOK TIME:** 11 minutes
**TOTAL TIME:** 21 minutes

# SQUASH AND KALE SALAD

*Another tasty salad with a hint of zing is this amazing autumn salad with squash, kale, and avocado. I love the combination of creamy and bright textures in this one.*

**1 medium delicata squash**

**olive oil spray**

**1 teaspoon Trader Joe's Everything but the Bagel Seasoning Blend**

**2 cups kale, chopped**

**1 cup cherry tomatoes, halved**

**1 large cucumber, chopped**

**¼ cup sunflower seeds**

**½ avocado, sliced**

**Trader Joe's Spicy Cashew Butter Dressing**

**YIELD: 6 SERVINGS**

Preheat the air fryer to 375°F. While that's heating up, slice the squash into strips lengthwise about 1-inch thick, then cut the slices in half lengthwise. Place the squash strips into a container with a lid, spray olive oil over the squash, then add the seasoning blend. Lightly toss to coat the squash with the seasoning and oil.

Place the squash in the air fryer basket and cook for 10 minutes. Shake the basket about halfway through.

While the squash is cooking, plate the three salad veggies evenly across 6 plates. When the squash is done cooking, let stand for 3 minutes, then add to the salad veggies. Sprinkle the sunflower seeds over the top, add the slices of avocado, then drizzle with the dressing. Serve immediately.

**PREP TIME:** 10 minutes
**COOK TIME:** 10 minutes
**TOTAL TIME:** 20 minutes

# BUFFALO GARBANZO GARDEN SALAD

*Here's a fun vegetarian twist on the Caesar salad, with a little punch, thanks to the Buffalo sauce both on the garbanzos and the salad itself.*

**1 (15-ounce) can Trader Joe's Organic Garbanzo Beans, drained and rinsed**

**1½ tablespoons plus ¼ cup Buffalo wing sauce**

**¼ teaspoon onion powder**

**½ teaspoon garlic powder**

**⅛ teaspoon ground black pepper**

**olive oil spray**

**2 heads of romaine, chopped**

**½ red onion, thinly sliced**

**2 green onions, diced**

**3 Roma tomatoes, chopped**

**¼ cup peeled, shredded carrots**

**3 radishes, thinly sliced**

**½ cup Trader Joe's Vegan Caesar Dressing or Organic Ranch Dressing**

**¼ cup Trader Joe's Crumbled Blue Cheese**

**¼ cup shredded parmesan cheese**

**YIELD: 4 TO 6 SERVINGS**

Preheat your air fryer to 400°F. While that's heating up, combine the garbanzo beans (garbanzos), the 11/2 tablespoons of Buffalo sauce, the onion and garlic powders, and black pepper to a small bowl. Use a spatula to coat the garbanzos thoroughly. Lightly spray the inside of the air fryer basket with olive oil spray, then put the coated garbanzos directly into the basket. Cook for 3 minutes, then shake the basket. Cook for another 3 minutes, shake the basket, and cook for another 3 minutes. Remove the garbanzos from the air fryer and set aside.

Combine the romaine, red onion, green onion, tomato, carrots, radish, remaining Buffalo sauce and Caesar (or Ranch) dressing in a large mixing bowl. Coat the veggies thoroughly with the sauces, then top with the garbanzos and the two kinds of cheese. Mix again, coating everything as evenly as possible, then plate and serve.

**PREP TIME:** 10 minutes
**COOK TIME:** 9 minutes
**TOTAL TIME:** 19 minutes

# Chapter 5

# SEAFOOD SAVORIES

# SUPER-SIMPLE SALMON

*So, I don't like fishy-tasting fish. Of course, that means fresh salmon is a favorite of mine. It's healthy, it's tasty, and, with an air fryer, it's super easy and fast. This particular recipe is a new favorite in our household.*

olive oil spray

approximately 1 pound Trader Joe's Atlantic Salmon boneless fillets

1 teaspoon granulated dried onion

1 teaspoon dried chives

½ teaspoon dried thyme

½ teaspoon dried rosemary

1 teaspoon garlic powder

lemon juice

**YIELD: 4 SERVINGS**

Preheat the air fryer to 400°F. Lightly spray the inside of your air fryer basket with olive oil. Rinse off the salmon fillets with cool water, then pat dry with paper towels. Set the salmon on a plate and lightly spray it with olive oil.

Next, pour the seasonings together into a jar, replace lid, and shake vigorously until the seasonings are all combined. Now sprinkle the seasonings over the salmon and gently rub into the flesh of the fish.

Place the salmon in the air fryer basket, without any of the fish overlapping. Cook at 400°F for 8 minutes. With a butter knife, check the doneness of the fish. If the fish is a little undercooked, use tongs to rearrange the fish and cook for an additional 2 to 3 minutes, as needed.

Top the salmon with lemon juice and serve immediately.

**PREP TIME:** 5 minutes
**COOK TIME:** 8 minutes
**TOTAL TIME:** 13 minutes

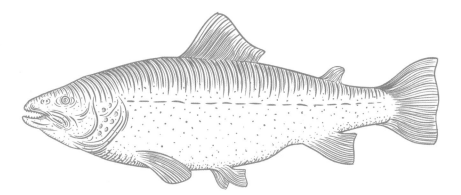

# ARGENTINIAN RED SHRIMP BUNS

*I've tried many types of buns and meat-stuffed rolls before, but I wanted to try something a little different. Combining the dough of a traditional doughy bun with the amazing Argentinian Shrimp from TJ's just felt like the right choice. Hopefully, you'll feel the same way when you make them.*

**1 cup warm water**

**3 tablespoons cane sugar**

**1 package dry yeast (approximately 2¼ teaspoons)**

**3¼ cups gluten-free all-purpose flour, plus extra for dusting**

**3 tablespoons olive oil**

**¼ teaspoon salt**

**olive oil spray**

**2 (9-ounce) packages Trader Joe's Argentinian Red Shrimp with Garlic Butter & Togarashi Style Seasoning, thawed, in the package, butter melted**

**YIELD: 10 TO 12 BUNS**

Combine the water, sugar, and yeast in a medium mixing bowl. Mix thoroughly, then cover and let stand for 5 minutes so the yeast can activate.

Once the yeast is activated, slowly add in the flour, oil, and salt to the yeast mixture. Stir together until a dough forms. Sprinkle a clean, dry surface with all-purpose flour, then remove the dough from the bowl and place on the floured surface. Knead the dough until it becomes smooth and elastic, about 10 minutes. Lightly spray with the olive oil spray the inside of a large mixing bowl and place the dough in to rise. Cover the bowl and let rise for 1 hour, or until the dough doubles in size.

Next, punch down the dough and let it rest for 5 minutes. Preheat the air fryer to 350°F. Divide the dough into 10 to 12 equal portions. Using your hands, make balls of the dough and set aside. Take one dough ball and roll it out on a floured surface until the dough disk is about ¼-inch thick. Repeat with the other dough balls.

In the center of each disk place a few shrimp and spoon a very small amount, approximately ¼ teaspoon, of the melted butter and seasoning over the shrimp, leaving enough dough at the edges to fold up around the filling. Fold the edges up and bring to the center. Pinch together and set aside. Repeat with the remaining dough disks.

Lightly spray olive oil in the air fryer basket and place the shrimp buns inside. Lightly spray with olive oil and cook for 7 to 10 minutes, or until the dough is golden-brown on top. Remove the buns from the air fryer and let stand for 5 minutes before serving.

**PREP TIME:** 30 minutes
**REST TIME:** 1 hour 5 minutes
**COOK TIME:** 7 to 10 minutes
**TOTAL TIME:** 1 hour 42 minutes to 1 hour 45 minutes

# SHRIMP SEAFOOD BURGERS

*Discovering these delicious shrimp burgers at TJ's was like a glorious discovery on a treasure hunt. Adding the pineapple salsa to them was the crown jewel.*

**olive or vegetable oil spray**

**1 package (4 patties) Trader Joe's Shrimp Seafood Burgers**

**4 wheat buns**

**lettuce**

**1 tomato, sliced**

**Trader Joe's Pineapple Salsa**

**YIELD: 4 BURGERS**

Preheat your air fryer to 400°F for 5 minutes. Lightly spray the basket with olive or vegetable oil. Place the patties in flat, not overlapping, and cook for 5 minutes. Flip them and cook for another 5 minutes.

While they're cooking, toast your wheat buns and prepare your lettuce and tomatoes. When the patties are done cooking, place them immediately on the toasted bread, add lettuce and tomato slices, and top with pineapple salsa. Serve immediately.

**PREP TIME:** 5 minutes
**COOK TIME:** 10 minutes
**TOTAL TIME:** 15 minutes

# CRAB CAKES

*Crab cakes are among those things that I absolutely, utterly adore. I don't eat them often, mostly because, well, they're a lot of work. Or, they were. Now that I use my air fryer, they're easy, fast, and delicious. And with this recipe, gluten free!*

**8 ounces Trader Joe's Wild Caught Crab Meat**

**¼ cup chopped red bell pepper**

**3 green onions, chopped**

**3 tablespoons Trader Joe's Chile Lime Mayonnaise**

**2 tablespoons gluten-free breadcrumbs**

**1 teaspoon Trader Joe's Green Goddess Seasoning Blend**

**olive oil spray**

**lemon wedges, for garnish (optional)**

**YIELD: 4 SERVINGS**

Combine all the ingredients except the oil spray and lemon in a medium bowl. Mash together to form a sticky mix. Pat the mix into 4 patties. Lightly spray the air fryer basket with olive oil, then cook at 370°F for 5 minutes. Flip the patties and cook for another 5 minutes. Remove from the air fryer and serve with lemon wedges, if using.

**PREP TIME:** 10 minutes
**COOK TIME:** 10 minutes
**TOTAL TIME:** 20 minutes

# GLUTEN-FREE COCONUT SHRIMP

*There's just something about coconut shrimp that makes my mouth water at the mention of them. Having to eat gluten free, however, I haven't found the option available to me much. Until I crafted this recipe for easy cooking in the air fryer.*

olive oil spray

½ cup Trader Joe's Organic Unsweetened Flake Coconut

1 teaspoon garlic powder

1 teaspoon onion powder

1 large egg, beaten

1 pound large shrimp, peeled

1 (8-ounce) package cream cheese, softened

1 to 2 tablespoons milk

10 ounces crushed pineapple, drained (about half a can)

**YIELD: 3 TO 4 SERVINGS**

Spray the air fryer basket with cooking spray. Combine the coconut and garlic and onion powder in a shallow bowl. Put the beaten egg in a separate bowl. Dip the shrimp in the egg first, then the coconut mixture. Immediately place the shrimp in the air fryer basket. Shrimp may be touching but not overlapping. Cook for 10 minutes at 350°F.

While the shrimp is cooking, combine the cream cheese, milk, and pineapple in a small bowl. Mix thoroughly until the cheese is smooth and the only chunks remaining are the pineapple. Remove the shrimp from the air fryer and let stand for 5 minutes before serving with the pineapple sauce.

**PREP TIME:** 10 minutes
**COOK TIME:** 10 minutes
**TOTAL TIME:** 20 minutes

# TRADER JOE'S COCONUT SHRIMP WITH PINEAPPLE SAUCE

For those who don't have to eat gluten free, TJ's provides you with these amazing coconut shrimp that are incredibly quick and easy to whip up. My contribution is this amazing pineapple sauce my family has loved for years. Enjoy!

olive oil spray

1 (12-ounce) package Trader Joe's Coconut Shrimp, frozen

1 (8-ounce) package cream cheese, softened

1 to 2 tablespoons milk

½ (20-ounce) can crushed pineapple, drained

**YIELD: 3 SERVINGS**

Preheat the air fryer to 400°F. Lightly spray the air fryer basket, then place the frozen shrimp in the basket and cook for 10 to 12 minutes. Remove when the shrimp is crispy and golden-brown.

While the shrimp is cooking, combine the cream cheese, milk, and pineapple in a small bowl. Mix thoroughly until the cheese is smooth and the only chunks remaining are the pineapple. Remove the shrimp from the air fryer and let stand for 5 minutes before serving with the pineapple sauce.

**PREP TIME:** 5 minutes
**COOK TIME:** 10 to 12 minutes
**TOTAL TIME:** 15 to 17 minutes

# CRISPY LOBSTER RAVIOLI

*I first had "crispy" ravioli while visiting St. Louis, where they enjoy the famous toasted ravioli. When I discovered the air fryer, I knew there had to be a way to enjoy something similar with the amazing lobster ravioli from TJ's. Instead of breading the ravioli though, I just crisped them up as is and discovered that's all they need to be amazing and crisp for dipping in my favorite TJ's marinara sauce.*

**6 cups water**

**1 (9-ounce) package Trader Giotto's Lobster Ravioli**

**your favorite Trader Joe's marinara sauce (I love Trader Giotto's Organic Tomato Basil Marinara Sauce and Trader Giotto's Traditional Marinara Sauce)**

**Trader Joe's Spices of the World 21 Seasoning Salute**

**olive oil spray**

**handful fresh cilantro, stemmed**

**4 lemon wedges**

**YIELD: 2 SERVINGS**

In a medium saucepan, set 6 cups of water to boil over medium heat. Preheat your air fryer to 400°F for 5 minutes. When the water reaches boiling, use a slotted spoon to add the ravioli in carefully. Let the ravioli cook for 3 to 5 minutes, then remove them with the slotted spoon, letting as much water drain away as possible.

Lay the ravioli on a plate and lightly spray with olive oil. Sprinkle lightly with 21 Seasoning Salute blend. Flip the ravioli, spraying again with olive oil and sprinkling on more seasoning.

Place the ravioli in the air fryer basket. Don't let them overlap so they all crisp evenly. Cook for 5 minutes. Remove the ravioli from the air fryer and let stand for 5 minutes before serving. Plate and garnish with fresh cilantro and lemon wedges, with marinara sauce for dipping.

**PREP TIME:** 3 to 5 minutes
**COOK TIME:** 13 to 18 minutes
**TOTAL TIME:** 16 to 23 minutes

# CAESAR SHRIMP SALAD

*Leafy greens are essential for our health. They provide us with that roughage our system needs to, well, stay happy, we'll just say. And if I can add in some shrimp to make those leafy greens even tastier? You better believe it's going to happen.*

2 romaine hearts, chopped

1 cup cherry tomatoes

1 pound uncooked shrimp, peeled

olive oil spray

¼ teaspoon ground black pepper

½ teaspoon paprika

½ teaspoon garlic powder

½ teaspoon dried chives

½ cup Trader Joe's Cassava Cauliflower Blend Baking Mix

1 tablespoon lemon juice

Trader Joe's Vegan Caesar Dressing

shredded parmesan cheese

**YIELD: 4 SERVINGS**

Put the romaine and tomatoes into the serving bowl you plan to use for the salad. Place in the fridge while you cook. Preheat the air fryer to 375°F. Put the shrimp into a container with a lid. Lightly spray olive oil over the shrimp, then add in the seasonings, baking mix, and lemon juice. Cover and shake to coat the shrimp thoroughly.

Lightly spray the inside of the air fryer basket with olive oil spray, then place the shrimp in the basket. Cook for 2 to 3 minutes or until lightly browned. Toss the shrimp to expose the uncooked sides. Spritz the shrimp with more olive oil and cook for another 2 to 3 minutes.

Remove the shrimp and toss it into the salad you made earlier, removed from the fridge. Sprinkle the parmesan cheese over it, then drizzle the dressing over the salad. Use tongs to mix the salad lightly, then serve.

**PREP TIME:** 5 minutes
**COOK TIME:** 4 to 6 minutes
**TOTAL TIME:** 9 to 11 minutes

# CAJUN SHRIMP AND SAUSAGE SKEWERS

*Another super-easy, delicious meal is this: spicy Cajun-style shrimp and sausage skewers. I love serving them with Cajun-style (or even Cuban-style) rice and beans for a savory meal the whole family can enjoy.*

**24 jumbo shrimp, cleaned and peeled**

**6 ounces Trader Joe's Sausage-less Sausage, sliced**

**1 small white onion, cut into large chunks**

**1 red bell pepper, cut into large chunks**

**2 tablespoons Cajun seasoning**

**olive oil spray**

**YIELD: 6 TO 10 SKEWERS**

Put the shrimp, sausage, onion, and bell pepper in a medium mixing bowl or container with a lid, sprinkling the seasoning over it. Toss the ingredients until thoroughly coated with the seasoning. Preheat the air fryer to 400°F for 5 minutes. While that's heating up, skewer the shrimp, sausage, onion, and pepper chunks. Spray air fryer basket with olive oil and place the skewers in it. Cook for 8 to 10 minutes, or until shrimp becomes opaque and veggies get blackened corners. Let stand for 3 to 5 minutes, and serve.

**PREP TIME:** 7 to 10 minutes
**COOK TIME:** 8 to 10 minutes
**TOTAL TIME:** 15 to 20 minutes

# ASIAN-INSPIRED MAHI-MAHI

*In case you couldn't tell by the many offerings in this cookbook, Asian-inspired anything is a win in my house. The more I cook with Asian ingredients and experiment with TJ's ingredients in that family, the more I love it. This particular recipe turned out to be simple, delicious fare that works as a great healthy staple for days I'm in a hurry without feeling like I'm neglecting my taste buds.*

**2 tablespoons unsalted butter, melted**

**2 teaspoons garlic powder**

**1 tablespoon Trader Joe's Nori Komi Furikake Japanese Multi-Purpose Seasoning**

**1 tablespoon Trader Joe's San Soyaki sauce**

**1 teaspoon onion powder**

**1 tablespoon lemon juice**

**3 or 4 mahi-mahi fillets, fresh (12 to 16 ounces)**

**YIELD: 3 OR 4 SERVINGS**

Preheat the air fryer to 360°F for 5 minutes. While that's heating up, combine all the ingredients, except for the fish, in a small bowl and blend thoroughly with a spoon or basting brush. Line an air fryer baking sheet with wax paper, then place the fish on the sheet, fillets side by side. With a basting brush, coat each fillet with the sauce blend. Cook the fillets for 12 to 15 minutes or until the fish is flaky when tested with a fork. Serve immediately.

**PREP TIME:** 5 minutes
**COOK TIME:** 12 to 15 minutes
**TOTAL TIME:** 17 to 20 minutes

# AMAZING CHILE LIME FISH CAKES

*I originally crafted a similar fish cakes recipe in honor of my grandmother's time in Bermuda on her flight around the world in 1964. I used a traditional Bermudan recipe as the foundation, then made it my own. Now, with TJ's ingredients and the air fryer, the recipe is even more amazing and super easy (and healthier!).*

1 cup water

1 pound fresh cod or tilapia

2½ cups cooked Trader Joe's Mashed Cauliflower

1 cup sweet peas, blanched

3 cloves garlic, minced

8 strips of bacon, cooked and crumbled

1 large egg

1 small white onion, chopped fine

¼ teaspoon ground black pepper

2 teaspoons Trader Joe's Chile Lime Seasoning Blend

gluten-free 1-to-1 flour

olive oil spray

**YIELD: 10 TO 12 FISH CAKES**

Pour water in a medium skillet, then add the fish. Cook over medium heat for 5 to 7 minutes, until the fish becomes softened and can be flaked with a fork. Once the fish is ready, remove it from the water and use a fork to flake it. Drain any liquid. Mix the flaked fish with the other ingredients, minus the oil and flour, in a large mixing bowl. In a separate bowl, place a thick layer of gluten-free flour for coating the fish cakes. Ball a hamburger patty–size amount of the fish and cauliflower mix with your hand or a spoon. Place it in a separate floured bowl.

Preheat the air fryer to 350°F. While that's heating up, flatten the ball into a patty and thoroughly coat all sides with the flour. Repeat with all the fish mix. Heavily spray the air fryer basket with olive oil, then carefully place the patties inside the basket, avoiding overlapping the patties. Cook for 7 to 10 minutes, then carefully flip the patties over and cook for another 7 minutes or until the patties are golden-brown all over. Remove from the air fryer and plate. Repeat with the remaining patties. Serve immediately.

**PREP TIME:** 20 minutes
**COOK TIME:** 19 to 36 minutes
**TOTAL TIME:** 39 to 56 minutes

# GREEN CURRY SHRIMP

*Trader Joe's green curry simmer sauce makes curry recipes so easy and fast. Just add coconut milk and some veggies and you've got the perfect meal every time.*

**3 cups jasmine rice**

**1 pound shrimp, peeled**

**⅓ cup coconut milk**

**4 tablespoons Trader Joe's Thai Green Curry Simmer Sauce**

**2 green onions, chopped**

**1 red bell pepper**

**1 teaspoon ground cumin**

**dash ground black pepper**

**½ cup Trader Joe's Organic Garbanzo Beans, rinsed and drained**

**YIELD: 4 SERVINGS**

Prepare the rice as directed on the package. While the rice is cooking, preheat the air fryer to 360°F. Lightly grease an air fryer pan and combine the other ingredients in the pan. Cook for 12 minutes. Shrimp should be opaque when cooked. If the shrimp need a few more minutes, cook in 2-minute increments until fully cooked. Let stand for 2 to 3 minutes before serving with rice.

**PREP TIME:** 5 minutes
**COOK TIME:** 12 minutes
**TOTAL TIME:** 17 minutes

Chapter 6

# MEAT ME AT THE FAIR

# BALSAMIC ROSEMARY AND MUSHROOM STEAK TIPS

*This one became an instant classic in our household—and I'm not particularly fond of steak myself. But that first bite sold me, and we will forever make this air fryer steak dinner with Trader Joe's ingredients, thanks to the way the seasonings of the marinade, the tenderness of the meat, and the deliciousness of the mashed cauliflower blend together for an indescribably delicious meal.*

**12 ounces Trader Joe's Mushroom Medley, frozen**

**1 to 1¼ pounds Trader Joe's Balsamic Rosemary Beef Steak Tips**

**1 pound Trader Joe's Mashed Cauliflower, prepared**

**YIELD: 6 SERVINGS**

Fill a large bowl with cold water and place the bag of Mushroom Medley in the water to partially thaw before cooking. While the mushrooms are thawing, preheat your air fryer to 400°F for 5 minutes.

Once the air fryer is ready, dump the Balsamic Rosemary Beef Steak Tips into an ungreased pan. Part the chunks of meat to help cook more thoroughly, then cook in the air fryer for 10 minutes.

Remove the pan from the air fryer and stir the steak tips a bit.

If you prefer medium-well-done steak, add the mushrooms, mixing them into the pan and coating them with the marinade from the steak, and cook for 10 minutes.

Now, if you prefer a well-done steak, return the pan to the air fryer and cook for another 10 minutes. Now, remove the pan from the air fryer, add the mushrooms, stirring them in and coating with the balsamic marinade, and return to the air fryer for another 10 minutes (totaling 30 minutes cook time).

While the steak tips are cooking, prepare your mashed cauliflower as directed on the package and cover until you're ready to serve.

When the meat/mushroom medley is done cooking, plate the mashed cauliflower, top it with the meat and mushrooms, and serve immediately.

**PREP TIME:** 5 minutes
**COOK TIME:** 20 to 30 minutes
**TOTAL TIME:** 25 to 35 minutes

# PEPPERCORN GARLIC PORK LOIN WITH PEPPER JELLY

*My husband isn't a fan of pork, at all—and he thought the idea of pepper jelly insane. "Who would eat that?" Then he met this recipe and changed his mind about both forever.*

**olive oil spray**

**1 package Trader Joe's Peppercorn-Garlic Boneless Pork Tenderloin**

**½ large white onion, chopped or sliced**

**Trader Joe's Hot & Sweet Pepper Jelly**

**YIELD: 4 SERVINGS**

Preheat the air fryer to 350°F for 5 minutes. Lightly spray a medium air fryer pan with olive oil, then place the tenderloin in the pan. If needed, cut in half or smaller chunks to speed up cooking time. Cook for 10 minutes.

Flip the meat over to expose the raw meat to the top of the air fryer. Cook for 10 minutes.

Now add the onion slices/chunks to the pan, and mix in with the pork and juices. Then cook for another 10 minutes.

Remove the pork from the air fryer and let stand for 5 minutes. Serve with pepper jelly on top.

**PREP TIME:** 5 minutes
**COOK TIME:** 30 minutes
**TOTAL TIME:** 35 minutes

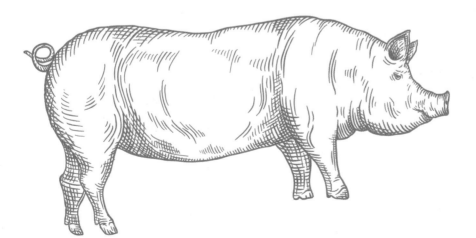

# SALAMI MUSHROOM CALZONES

*Calzones are a favorite in our household, so when I remembered that there's this incredible premade pizza dough at TJ's, I knew I had to turn it into a calzone. I wanted something a little different from the usual toppings (stuffings?), too, so instead of going for pepperoni, I pulled out the salami and the mushroom medley. Wow. Those ingredients sent this over the top.*

**flour, for rolling**

**16 ounces Trader Giotto's Ready to Bake Garlic & Herb Pizza Dough**

**2 tablespoons Trader Giotto's Fat Free Pizza Sauce**

**8 to 10 slices of Trader Joe's Salame di Parma Mild Salami**

**2 handfuls Trader Joe's Mushroom Medley, thawed**

**¼ cup feta cheese, divided**

**½ teaspoon garlic powder, divided**

**½ teaspoon Italian seasoning, divided**

**olive oil spray (optional)**

**YIELD: 2 LARGE CALZONES**

On a clean, dry, flat surface, sprinkle some flour. Split the dough in half and ball into two balls. Put one dough ball on the floured surface and set the other aside. Roll out the ball flat to about ⅓ of an inch thick all the way around.

Spread 1 tablespoon pizza sauce on the middle portion of the dough. Lay in slices of salami and mushrooms, then sprinkle on the cheese. Now sprinkle on the garlic powder and Italian seasoning.

Next, fold the sides of the dough up over the pile of goodies in the middle and pinch together. Then fold up the ends and pinch together.

Carefully lift the calzone and place it flat into the basket on a sheet of parchment paper or silicone liner in the air fryer. If you don't have a liner, lightly spray the basket with olive oil.

Cook for 10 minutes, then remove and let stand for 5 minutes before serving.

Repeat the process for the other calzone.

**PREP TIME:** 7 to 10 minutes
**COOK TIME:** 10 minutes
**TOTAL TIME:** 17 to 20 minutes

# FAST AND FLAVORFUL CABERNET BEEF ROAST WITH VEGGIES

*Pot roast is not remotely my husband's favorite meal. In fact, he'd be happy to never taste the stuff again. That is, until he tasted this roast. Trader Joe's Cabernet beef, as you probably already know, is a one-of-a-kind study in deliciousness and making it as a simple roast is always a pleasure.*

**2 pounds Trader Joe's Cabernet Beef Pot Roast**

**4 carrots, peeled and chopped**

**2 onions, chopped**

**½ pound green beans**

**½ cup beef stock**

**YIELD: 4 TO 6 SERVINGS**

Preheat your air fryer to 350°F for 5 minutes. Cut the roast in half, then place it, with the drippings from the package, in a medium air fryer pan. Add the veggies and beef stock. Cook for 10 minutes.

At this point, flip the meat and larger veggies to expose the other sides to the top of the pan, and ladle the fluids in the pan over the meat and veggies. Cook for another 10 minutes. Rotate the meat and veggies again, ladling the liquid over everything again, then cook for another 10 minutes. Let stand for 5 minutes, then serve.

**PREP TIME:** 5 to 7 minutes
**COOK TIME:** 30 minutes
**TOTAL TIME:** 35 to 37 minutes

# SHAWARMA BEEF AND CAULIFLOWER BOWL

*This delicious, easy meal is another winner, thanks to Trader Joe's amazing premade meat marinades. The combination of this amazing meat with the quinoa dish with a Moroccan twist makes this one of the best things ever done with beef—in my humble opinion, anyway.*

**2 cups quinoa, uncooked**

**1½ pounds Trader Joe's Shawarma Beef Sirloin**

**3 teaspoons garlic powder**

**1 teaspoon ground cumin**

**1 teaspoon curry powder**

**½ teaspoon anise seeds**

**1 teaspoon ground cinnamon**

**½ teaspoon ground black pepper**

**½ teaspoon cayenne pepper**

**¼ cup roasted, unsalted sunflower seeds**

**¼ cup Trader Joe's Nuts Raw Sliced Almonds**

**2 tablespoons water**

**4 cups cauliflower pieces, frozen**

**¾ cup prunes or dates, chopped**

**YIELD: 6 TO 8 SERVINGS**

Preheat the air fryer to 350°F for 5 minutes. Prepare the quinoa as directed on the package.

Place the beef with the juices in a medium air fryer pan and cook for 15 minutes. Rotate the meat, exposing the uncooked portions to the top and cook for another 15 minutes.

Once the quinoa starts to boil and plump up, add all the seasonings and sunflower seeds and almond slices. Stir consistently and let it cook down a bit. Then add water, cauliflower, and prunes or dates and stir thoroughly. Cover the pan and let simmer on low heat for 10 minutes.

Remove the beef from the air fryer and plate with quinoa-veggie mix, pouring some of the sauce from the air fryer pan over each plate. Serve immediately.

**PREP TIME:** 5 minutes
**COOK TIME:** 30 minutes
**TOTAL TIME:** 35 minutes

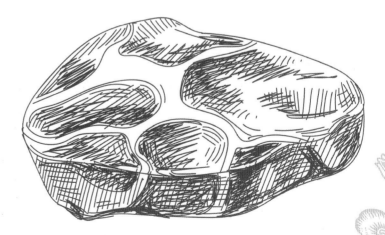

# SHAWARMA BEEF MEAT PIE

*I'm always looking for new, wonderful ways to use Trader Joe's meaty offerings. I happen to adore these shawarma beef meat pies, so the marriage of the two seemed like a great fit. And using the premade crusts make it a super-easy project, too.*

**1½ pounds Trader Joe's Shawarma Beef Sirloin**

**2 russet potatoes, peeled and cubed**

**1 (22-ounce) package Trader Joe's Pie Crusts, thawed**

**1 cup green beans, trimmed and cut**

**1 large carrot, peeled and shredded**

**½ cup Trader Joe's Organic Beef Bone Broth**

**2 teaspoons ground black pepper**

**2 teaspoons ground allspice**

**3 teaspoons garlic powder**

**½ teaspoon ground cloves**

**½ teaspoon ground cinnamon**

**½ teaspoon ground nutmeg**

**½ teaspoon ground cardamom**

**¼ teaspoon chili powder**

**½ teaspoon dried oregano**

**¼ teaspoon salt**

**olive oil, for basting**

**YIELD: 4 POT PIES**

Preheat the air fryer to 350°F. Place the beef with the juices and the potato cubes in a medium air fryer pan and cook for 15 minutes. Rotate the meat, exposing the uncooked portions to the top, and cook for another 10 minutes. The meat should be slightly undercooked when you remove it now.

While the meat and potatoes are cooking, roll out each pie crust on a lightly floured surface to about ¼-inch thickness, then cut each into four sections. Lightly grease 4 ramekins and line with 4 pieces of the pie crust.

Next, combine the meat, potatoes, veggies, bone broth, and seasonings in a large bowl and mix together, coating everything thoroughly. Now fill the lined ramekins with the filling and use the remaining 4 sections of pie crust to top the pies. Trim off excess crust. Poke a few small holes in the top of the crusts. Baste the tops of the crusts lightly with olive oil.

Now raise the temperature to 400°F on the air fryer and place the ramekins in the air fryer. Cook for 15 minutes or until the crusts turn golden-brown. Remove from the air fryer and let stand for 5 minutes before serving.

**PREP TIME:** 15 minutes
**COOK TIME:** 40 minutes
**TOTAL TIME:** 55 minutes

# AUSSIE-STYLE SAUSAGE ROLLS

*Since my first visit to Australia back in 2008, I've been in love with Aussie-style sausage rolls. I've occasionally found them for sale in the USA, but rarely—and never gluten free. So, if you're anything like me, you'll appreciate this easy, delicious, and homemade air fryer option that you can make with regular or gluten-free flour.*

## FOR THE FILLING

½ tablespoon olive oil

2 cloves garlic, minced

1 small yellow onion, chopped fine

2 celery stalks, chopped fine

1 pound ground sweet Italian sausage

2 teaspoons fennel seeds

¾ cup gluten-free breadcrumbs

1 egg

1 teaspoon ground black pepper

## FOR THE ROLLS

1 (18.3-ounce) package Trader Joe's All Butter Puff Pastry

2 eggs, lightly whisked, divided

olive oil spray

tomato sauce or ketchup, for serving

**YIELD: 8 SAUSAGE ROLLS**

Heat the oil in a medium nonstick skillet over medium heat. Add the garlic, onion, and celery to the pan and sauté for 4 minutes, or until golden-brown. Transfer the ingredients to a large bowl, set aside, and let cool for 10 minutes.

Now add the remaining filling ingredients to the bowl and use your hands to work everything together. Set aside.

Roll out the puff pastry sheets and brush the egg along both of the longer sides of the pastries. Evenly distribute the filling between the sheets, at the center of the dough. Shape the meat into a log, making sure the meat is compact and tight, no gaps. Now roll the pastry up around the meat and seal shut with another egg wash. Wrap in wax paper and chill for 1 hour.

Preheat the air fryer to 350°F. Lightly spray air fryer baking sheets with olive oil. Remove the pastry from the fridge and place on the air fryer baking sheet. Cut the rolls into 4 sections each. Brush the rolls with more egg, then cook for 25 minutes or until the pastry turns deep golden-brown.

Let cool for 5 minutes on the baking sheets, then serve with tomato sauce or ketchup.

**PREP TIME:** 10 minutes
**COOK TIME:** 29 minutes
**TOTAL TIME:** 39 minutes

# CABERNET BEEF TARTS

*For another easy, hearty meal, perfect for autumn, winter, and early spring, beef tarts come on the scene. The rich, red Cabernet turns the meat tender and intriguing, too, making these tarts an amazing option for casual dinner parties or easy meals with the family.*

**1 pound Trader Joe's Cabernet Beef Pot Roast**

**3 medium carrots, peeled and chopped**

**1 large white onion, chopped**

**1 tablespoon red wine vinegar**

**¼ cup beef stock**

**2 tablespoons all-purpose flour**

**1 (18.3-ounce) package Trader Joe's All Butter Puff Pastry**

**YIELD: 4 TARTS**

Preheat the air fryer to 350°F. While it's heating up, cube the beef and place it in a large air fryer pan with the packaged drippings and marinade. Cook for 10 minutes, then use tongs to flip the meat to expose the undercooked sides. Cook for another 10 minutes.

While the beef is cooking, put the carrots, onion, red wine vinegar, beef stock, and flour in a large mixing bowl, and combine thoroughly. When the beef is done cooking, add it to the bowl with other ingredients and mix to coat the beef. Set aside.

Lay out the puff pastry sheets on a flat surface. Cut each sheet into quarters. Place 4 pieces of pastry dough into lightly greased ramekins and press the dough into the sides and bottom. Now take the beef and veggie mixture and fill the dough cups. Next, place the other 4 pieces as tops to the beef tarts and press in. Put the ramekins in the air fryer and cook for 10 to 12 minutes or until the pastry is golden-brown. Remove from the air fryer and let stand 5 minutes before serving.

**PREP TIME:** 15 minutes
**COOK TIME:** 30 to 32 minutes
**TOTAL TIME:** 45 to 47 minutes

# BEEF ENCHILADAS

*I've always loved enchiladas: the spiciness mixed with the floury tortilla taste, the veggies, and the cheese. Preparing enchiladas with amazing beef in an air fryer only makes them better.*

**4 cups canned diced tomatoes**

**8 tablespoons Trader Joe's Honey Aleppo Sauce**

**2 teaspoons garlic powder**

**2 teaspoons dried minced onion**

**1 teaspoon ground black pepper**

**2 tablespoons ground cumin**

**approximately 2 pounds Trader Joe's Cabernet Beef Pot Roast**

**flour tortillas**

**shredded Mexican-style or cheddar cheese**

**YIELD: 8 TO 10 ENCHILADAS**

In a medium bowl with a lid, combine the diced tomatoes, Aleppo sauce, and seasonings. Cover and let rest in the refrigerator for an hour.

When it's time to cook, preheat the air fryer to 350°F for 5 minutes. While the air fryer is heating, cut the Cabernet beef into chunks for faster cooking. Cook for 10 minutes.

Now flip the meat, revealing the undercooked sides. Cook for another 10 minutes.

Next, remove the sauce you created earlier and let stand while you're cutting the beef into bite-size portions. The meat should still be a little pink in the middle to avoid overcooking. Plate the tortillas and spread the enchilada sauce evenly across the middle of each tortilla. Sprinkle on the cheese, then add the beef. Tuck the tortillas around the fillings, including the ends, and carefully place them in the air fryer basket, folded sides down. Cook for 5 minutes, then remove. Top with additional sauce and serve immediately.

**PREP TIME:** 5 to 7 minutes
**REST TIME:** 1 hour
**COOK TIME:** 25 minutes
**TOTAL TIME:** 1 hour 30 minutes to 1 hour 32 minutes

# CARNE ASADA TACOS

*My husband says there are four major food groups: pizza, tacos, ice cream, and doughnuts. Here's a new, simple, and delicious favorite of his for that second food group!*

half white onion, sliced

1½ pounds Trader Joe's Carne Asada Autentica beef

6 large tortillas

Trader Joe's Red Pepper Spread with Eggplant & Garlic

2 cups lettuce, chopped

2 tomatoes, chopped

½ cup shredded Mexican-style cheese

**YIELD: 6 LARGE TACOS**

Preheat the air fryer to 375°F. Place the sliced onion in an air fryer pan, along with the beef on top. Cook for 10 minutes. Rotate the meat and onions and cook for another 10 minutes.

Lay out the tortillas on plates and spread the red pepper spread evenly across them. Layer in the lettuce and tomato. Remove the beef and onions from the pan and cut the beef into bite-size chunks. Place the meat and onions into the tortillas and top with cheese. Serve immediately.

**PREP TIME:** 10 minutes
**COOK TIME:** 20 minutes
**TOTAL TIME:** 30 minutes

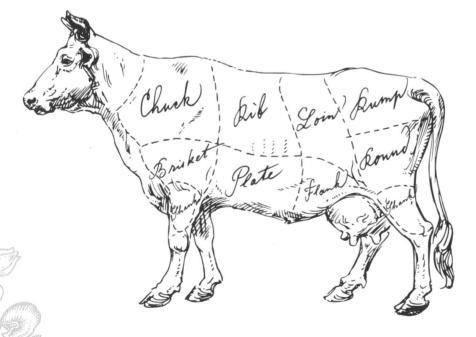

# PORK FAJITAS

*In my family, we grew up eating Tex-Mex before it was cool. Fajitas, burritos, tacos—they were a regular part of our weekly meal plan. So, when I found the pork carnitas at Trader Joe's, I knew I had to make something scrumptious with it.*

1 tablespoon olive oil

1 large white onion, sliced

2 red bell peppers, sliced

2 green bell peppers, sliced

1 teaspoon minced garlic

1 teaspoon ground cumin

1 teaspoon cayenne pepper

12 ounces Trader Joe's Traditional Carnitas

6 flour tortillas

**YIELD: 6 FAJITAS**

Pour olive oil into a medium skillet and warm over medium-low heat for 2 minutes. Add the onion, red and green peppers, garlic, and seasonings and cook in the oil for 3 minutes, stirring constantly.

Preheat the air fryer to 350°F. Next, place the carnitas meat in a medium air fryer pan and cook in the air fryer for 3 minutes.

While the meat is cooking, remove the veggie mix from the stove. Place the tortillas on a microwave-safe plate. Warm the tortillas in the microwave for 30 seconds.

Mix the meat in with the veggies, making sure you keep all that oil and spices and the sauce from the meat in there. Serve with the tortillas immediately.

**PREP TIME:** 5 minutes
**COOK TIME:** 8 minutes
**TOTAL TIME:** 13 minutes

# SPINACH TORTELLINI WITH ITALIAN SAUSAGE

*What's better than Trader Joe's Spinach Tortellini? Crispy tortellini with sausage and Alfredo sauce, that's what! The dish is perfect as a romantic dinner for two or an easy, casual meal before dashing out to meet up with friends.*

**2 pieces Trader Joe's Sausage-less Sausage**

**6 cups water**

**10 ounces Trader Giotto's Spinach Tortellini**

**½ cup Trader Giotto's Alfredo Pasta Sauce or Trader Joe's Cajun Style Alfredo Sauce**

**olive oil spray**

**handful of Trader Joe's Sun-Dried Tomatoes, for garnish**

**fresh basil, for garnish**

**YIELD: 2 SERVINGS**

Preheat the air fryer to 375°F for 5 minutes. While that's heating up, slice the sausage into bite-size pieces. When the air fryer is ready, toss in the sausage pieces and cook for 5 minutes.

While the sausage is cooking, boil 6 cups of water. With a slotted spoon, lower the tortellini into the water and let cook for 3 minutes. This will help the pasta cook better and crisp up in the air fryer.

With the slotted spoon, remove the tortellini to a medium plate or bowl and lightly spray with olive oil. Transfer the pasta to the air fryer basket with the sausage and cook for 5 minutes.

When done cooking, the pasta should be slightly crisp and the sausage browned. If the pasta isn't quite ready, toss the ingredients in the basket and cook for another 3 to 5 minutes. Transfer to two plates.

Immediately ladle on your Alfredo sauce and garnish with sun-dried tomatoes and fresh basil.

**PREP TIME:** 3 to 5 minutes
**COOK TIME:** 11 to 13 minutes
**TOTAL TIME:** 14 to 18 minutes

# RED WINE CHILI WITH CABERNET BEEF

*I don't know about you, but I love a good chili. A good chili with rich, dark flavors? Even better. This one has it all with rich tomatoes, dark red kidney beans, red wine, and, of course, Trader Joe's amazing Cabernet Beef!*

1 yellow onion, thinly sliced

1 fresh red chile, chopped

1 red bell pepper, chopped

1 (28-ounce) can diced tomatoes

2 tablespoons tomato paste

1 tablespoon olive oil

1 pound Trader Joe's Cabernet Beef Pot Roast, minced

½ teaspoon salt

¼ teaspoon ground black pepper

2 teaspoons chili powder

2 teaspoons ground cumin

1¼ cups water

2 to 4 tablespoons red wine

15 ounces dark red kidney beans, rinsed and drained

**YIELD: 5 TO 6 SERVINGS**

Preheat the air fryer to 360°F for 5 minutes. In a pot for the air fryer, combine the onion, chile, bell pepper, diced tomatoes, and tomato paste. Drizzle with the olive oil, then cook for 5 minutes. Next, add the minced beef to the pan, incorporating thoroughly, and cook for 5 minutes. The meat should be browned all over.

Now mix in the seasonings, water, and red wine, stirring together with the other ingredients, until well incorporated. Cook for another 10 minutes. Finally, add the kidney beans and then cook for 25 minutes. Stir thoroughly every 10 minutes until done. Let stand for 3 to 5 minutes, then serve with crackers, toast, or plain rice.

**PREP TIME:** 5 minutes
**COOK TIME:** 45 minutes
**TOTAL TIME:** 50 minutes

# CABERNET BEEF STEW

*Stew is one of those meals that just hits the right spot all autumn and winter—even spring—long. Thick, rich, meaty, delicious. Notch it up with the potato flakes for added thickness and I'd be happy to eat stew pretty much every day!*

1 tablespoon tomato paste

2 cups red wine

approximately 2 pounds Trader Joe's Cabernet Beef Pot Roast, cubed

1 teaspoon salt

1 teaspoon ground black pepper

3 tablespoons olive oil

½ cup mashed potato flakes

1 large Vidalia onion, chopped

4 cloves garlic, minced

2 carrots, peeled and diced

2 stalks celery, diced

½ cup water

**YIELD: 6 SERVINGS**

Preheat the air fryer to 350° for 5 minutes. Put the tomato paste and red wine in a large mixing bowl. Mix together until the paste has thinned and smoothed out in the wine. Add the meat and all the liquid contents of the package, then mix in the seasonings, the olive oil, and the mashed potato flakes. Next, add the onion, garlic, carrots, and celery and mix together.

Carefully pour the stew into your air fryer pot and cook for 25 minutes. The stew will have cooked down a bit, so add ½ cup water (or twice that, if a "soupy" texture is desired). Cook for another 5 to 10 minutes, depending on desired doneness of meat. Let stand for 5 minutes, then serve.

**PREP TIME:** 10 minutes
**COOK TIME:** 30 to 35 minutes
**TOTAL TIME:** 40 to 45 minutes

# BEEF RAMEN

*Before watching* The Ramen Girl, *starring Brittany Murphy, I had no idea ramen was a thing. I thought it was just something we called those noodles generically and served up in our weird family's traditional way with pineapple, soy sauce, veggies, and meat. Since the movie, I've been fascinated with real ramen and what it takes to be a chef. I'm still far from making it, but I hope you'll still enjoy this scrumptious take on the meal.*

**approximately ½ pound Trader Joe's Bool Kogi**

**6 cups water**

**1 package ramen-style noodles (3 to 5 ounces)**

**1 cup frozen peas**

**¼ white onion, sliced**

**1 teaspoon garlic powder**

**1 teaspoon ground ginger**

**1 tablespoon soy sauce**

**YIELD: 2 SERVINGS**

Preheat your air fryer to 350°F for 5 minutes. When the air fryer is ready, place the beef bool kogi in the basket and cook for 10 minutes. Flip the meat and repeat cooking for another 10 minutes. Make sure the meat is still a little red in the middle as you slice it for placement in the ramen.

While the meat is cooking, pour 6 cups of water into a medium saucepan. Bring to a boil over medium heat. When the water reaches boiling, add the ramen-style noodles and cook until soft, about 2 minutes. Remove from the heat and pour off about ⅓ of the water. Slice the meat thinly into 6 to 8 slices and place the meat in the saucepan. Add in the frozen peas, the onion, and the seasoning, stirring everything together. Cook for 5 minutes over medium heat. Now add in the soy sauce and let simmer for 5 minutes. Serve immediately.

**PREP TIME:** 5 minutes
**COOK TIME:** 20 to 30 minutes
**TOTAL TIME:** 25 to 35 minutes

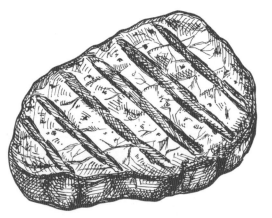

# Chapter 7

# THOSE FOWL CHOICES

# EASY KUNG PAO CHICKEN

*If you're looking for a super-simple Asian dish, this is the thing. Seriously. So delicious and easy. My family eats it as is, but you can also serve it over rice, rice noodles, or ramen for a starchy boost to keep the energy going.*

**olive oil spray**

**1 (23-ounce) package Trader Ming's Kung Pao Chicken, frozen**

**4 cups cooked rice, rice noodles, or ramen (your choice!)**

**YIELD: 4 SERVINGS**

Preheat your air fryer to 400°F for 5 minutes. If you're planning to cook rice, start the rice now, preparing as the package instructs.

Once the air fryer is preheated, remove the basket and insert your air fryer pan. Lightly spray the inside of the pan with olive oil. Remove the ingredients from the package and dump the chicken into the pan. Cut open the various packets and pour them into the pan with the chicken, saving the sauce for last. Then squeeze the sauce as evenly over the contents as possible.

Use a spoon or fork to mix the ingredients together. Return the basket to the air fryer and cook for 10 minutes. If you're cooking rice noodles or ramen, put the water on to boil now.

Remove the pan from the air fryer and use a wooden or bamboo spoon to mix the ingredients together again. Return to the air fryer and cook for another 7 to 10 minutes. Remove it and let stand for 5 minutes. Finish preparing your rice or noodles during this time, then serve the chicken over the bed of starch, approximately 1 cup per person of both the rice/noodles and the chicken mix.

**PREP TIME:** 3 to 4 minutes
**COOK TIME:** 17 to 20 minutes
**TOTAL TIME:** 20 to 24 minutes

# CHICKEN SPRING ROLLS AND VEGGIE FRIED RICE

*This meal is about as simple as they come. Easy spring rolls, easy rice. An all-in-one dinner the whole family will love, ready in about 10 minutes.*

vegetable or olive oil spray

**16 ounces Trader Joe's Vegetable Fried Rice**

**9 ounces Trader Joe's Chicken Spring Rolls**

**Trader Joe's Sweet Chili Sauce or Trader Ming's Gyoza Dipping Sauce**

**YIELD: 5 SERVINGS**

Preheat the air fryer to 350°F for 5 minutes. Lightly spray a large air fryer pan with vegetable oil or olive oil and pour the fried rice into the pan. If your air fryer is large enough, place the pan of rice in and lay the spring rolls out over it, not overlapping. Cook both together for 5 minutes. Otherwise, cook each for 5 minutes (total time: 10 minutes).

When they're ready, plate the ingredients together and serve with either the chili sauce or dipping sauce—or some other favorite Asian sauce.

**PREP TIME:** 5 minutes
**COOK TIME:** 5 to 10 minutes
**TOTAL TIME:** 10 to 15 minutes

# SPICY CHILE LIME CHICKEN FAJITAS

*Fajitas are always a winner in our household. They're delicious and oh-so-easy to make. This particular recipe adds a marinade, not something our family's typical fajitas include, making it an even more scrumptious choice for a quick meal.*

**2 teaspoons olive oil**

**2 tablespoons lime juice**

**2 teaspoons Trader Joe's Chile Lime Seasoning Blend**

**2 boneless, skinless chicken breasts, chopped into bite-size chunks**

**2 orange bell peppers, sliced thin**

**1 red onion, sliced thin**

**1 jalapeño, seeded and chopped fine**

**4 flour tortillas**

**handful fresh cilantro, chopped (optional)**

**lime wedges, for garnish (optional)**

**YIELD: 4 FAJITAS**

Put all the ingredients, except the tortillas, cilantro, and lime wedges into a bag or container you can seal. Seal it shut, then shake vigorously, coating the chicken and veggies thoroughly. Press any air out of the bag and reseal, then place in the fridge to chill for 1 hour.

Preheat your air fryer to 360°F. Put the chicken, veggies, and marinade in an air fryer pan and cook for 15 minutes. Flip the chicken and cook for an additional 10 minutes or until the interior temperature hits 165°F.

While the chicken is cooking, plate your tortillas. Once the chicken is ready, remove it from the air fryer and equally portion the chicken and veggies across the four tortillas. Let stand for 5 minutes, then garnish with fresh cilantro and lime wedges, if using.

**PREP TIME:** 10 minutes
**REST TIME:** 1 hour
**COOK TIME:** 25 minutes
**TOTAL TIME:** 1 hour 35 minutes

# GLUTEN-FREE CHICKEN PESTO PALM PASTA DELIGHT

*Chicken, pesto, heart of palm pasta. You can't get better than this for an easy, delicious meal any gluten-free gal can love.*

approximately 2 pounds Trader Joe's Pesto Genovese Chicken Breast

olive oil spray

2 (9-ounce) packages Trader Joe's Hearts of Palm pasta

6 teaspoons olive oil

**YIELD: 6 SERVINGS**

Preheat the air fryer to 400° for 5 minutes. Put the pesto chicken breast in a medium air fryer pan. Spray with olive oil spray and cook for 15 minutes. With a fork, move the chicken breast around, exposing the uncooked portions and bringing them to the top of the fryer. Cook for an additional 10 minutes.

When the chicken has about 7 minutes left, pour the contents of the hearts of palm pasta into a medium skillet. Stir constantly, cooking the pasta until the pasta is tender, 3 to 5 minutes.

Plate the pasta and top with the chicken and pesto sauce. Drizzle 1 teaspoon of olive oil over each serving. Serve immediately.

**PREP TIME:** 3 to 5 minutes
**COOK TIME:** 30 minutes
**TOTAL TIME:** 33 to 35 minutes

# BBQ CHICKEN TERIYAKI STIR-FRY WITH RICE NOODLES

*Whether that's a toss-it-in-from-the-freezer packet, a simple stir-fry, or homemade sushi, Asian cuisine is our favorite. And Trader Joe's ingredients just make it all better (and easier). This is a new favorite, easy go-to for a casual evening in.*

**8 ounces stir-fry rice noodles**

**olive oil spray**

**1 (21-ounce) package Trader Joe's BBQ Chicken Teriyaki, frozen**

**olive oil**

**2 teaspoons sesame oil**

**½ white onion, sliced thin**

**1 cup frozen peas and cauliflower or 2 cups large florets of broccoli or similar larger veggies pieces**

**½ cup fresh or canned crushed pineapple**

**½ cup Trader Joe's San Soyaki sauce**

**sesame seeds, for garnish (optional)**

**YIELD: 6 SERVINGS**

Prepare the rice noodles as the package recommends.

Lightly spray the air fryer basket with olive oil and place chicken in an air fryer pan with 1 packet of sauce. Reserve the second packet. Cook for 10 minutes.

While the chicken is cooking, add just enough olive oil to a medium skillet to coat the bottom. Add sesame oil to the skillet and heat for 1 to 2 minutes on low. Next, add the onion and coat with oil. (Be sure to do this in order or you'll find popping oil in your face! Trust me. I know!) Add half the reserved sauce packet to the pan. Blend with oil and onions.

Now add the frozen veggies, half of the noodles, the pineapple, and the reserved sauce. Coat everything, then add the remainder of the noodles and San Soyaki sauce. Cook for another 5 to 7 minutes, until veggies are cooked through and soft.

Plate the noodles-and-veggies mixture and evenly distribute chicken across the plates. Garnish with sesame seeds, if using, and top with extra any sauce from the pan.

**PREP TIME:** 5 minutes
**COOK TIME:** 10 to 15 minutes
**TOTAL TIME:** 15 to 20 minutes

# GREEN CURRY CHICKEN

*Curry is a staple in our house—has been since my earliest memories of dining with Grandma. She introduced me to all the authentic Indian foods she made while in India, as well as those she made with her close Indian friends who'd moved to Ohio near her. So, though the TJ's curry choices are primarily Thai-based, I've learned to love using them in easy, quick recipes too, giving my curry-loving heart a much easier time of it.*

**2 boneless, skinless chicken breasts**

**2 teaspoons olive oil**

**½ teaspoon ground cumin**

**1 teaspoon garlic powder**

**4 tablespoons Trader Joe's Thai Green Curry Simmer Sauce**

**2 cups jasmine rice**

**½ small white onion, sliced thin**

**1 red bell pepper, sliced thin**

**2 tablespoons unsalted, dry-roasted peanuts**

**YIELD: 2 SERVINGS**

Put the chicken, olive oil, seasonings, and the curry sauce in a plastic zipper bag or container with a lid. Seal the container or bag and shake vigorously, coating the chicken thoroughly with the marinade. Place in the fridge and let it rest for 1 hour.

Prepare the jasmine rice as usual and set aside. Preheat the air fryer to 360°F. Remove the chicken from the fridge and dump it and the marinade into an air fryer pan. Cook for 10 minutes. Using tongs or a fork, flip the chicken over to expose the undercooked side. Cook for 5 minutes, then add the vegetables and peanuts. Cook for another 5 to 7 minutes or until the interior of the chicken reaches 165°F. Remove from the air fryer and let stand 5 minutes before plating in 2 portions and serving with the rice.

**PREP TIME:** 5 minutes
**REST TIME:** 1 hour
**COOK TIME:** 20 to 22 minutes
**TOTAL TIME:** 1 hour 25 to 1 hour 27 minutes

# CHICKEN CURRY POT PIE

*I'd never thought of making a curry pot pie before this summer. But as I dug through the many amazing ingredients at Trader Joe's, I realized this could be a fantastic twist on this family favorite. Now I love serving this dish to our more adventurous guests when they pop in for a bite.*

2 tablespoons unsalted butter, melted

½ large yellow onion, chopped

½ green apple, peeled and chopped

3 Medjool dates, chopped

1 small zucchini, peeled and diced

1 medium carrot, peeled and diced

2 large red potatoes, chopped

1 teaspoon garlic powder

1½ teaspoons ground ginger

1 tablespoon Trader Joe's Curry Powder

1 tablespoon all-purpose flour, plus more for dusting

1 cup low-sodium chicken broth

½ tablespoon cornstarch

1 large boneless, skinless chicken breast, cooked and chopped

1 (18.3-ounce) package Trader Joe's All Butter Puff Pastry

1 large egg, lightly beaten

olive oil spray

**YIELD: 4 POT PIES**

Preheat the air fryer to 400°F. While that's heating up, combine all ingredients except the pastry and egg in a large mixing bowl. Mix thoroughly, making sure chicken and vegetables are completely coated. Lightly spray olive oil in 4 ramekins. Lay both sheets of puff pastry on a flat, dry surface and cut each into quarters. Press 1 quarter into each of the ramekins.

Fill the crusts with the chicken-and-vegetable filling mixture. Baste egg over the remaining 4 squares and then cover the pot pies with the squares. Place in the air fryer and cook for 15 to 17 minutes, or until the tops are golden-brown.

Remove the ramekins from the air fryer and let stand 5 minutes before serving.

**PREP TIME:** 10 minutes
**COOK TIME:** 15 to 17 minutes
**TOTAL TIME:** 25 to 27 minutes

# TOMATO EGGPLANT CHICKEN PASTA

*If you're looking to mix up your pasta game a little, I highly recommend this little recipe. It doesn't take much effort or time and is absolutely delicious, thanks to TJ's eggplant with tomatoes and onions. A giant, serious yum here.*

**2 cups bow-tie or rotini pasta**

**1 tablespoon unsalted butter, melted**

**½ teaspoon minced garlic**

**½ teaspoon Italian seasoning**

**2 small boneless, skinless chicken breasts**

**1 (9.9-ounce) container Trader Joe's Grecian Style Eggplant with Tomatoes & Onions**

**parmesan cheese**

**YIELD: 2 SERVINGS**

Prepare the pasta as the package directions indicate. While that's cooking, preheat your air fryer to 360°F. Combine the melted butter, garlic, and Italian seasoning in a small bowl, blending together. Brush the chicken breasts with the seasoned butter, then place them in the air fryer basket. Cook for 10 minutes, then flip and cook for another 10 to 12 minutes.

Plate the pasta evenly across two plates. Open the can of eggplant and spoon half of the can onto each pile of pasta. Top with the chicken breast, then sprinkle some parmesan cheese across each. Serve and enjoy.

**PREP TIME:** 5 minutes
**COOK TIME:** 20 to 22 minutes
**TOTAL TIME:** 25 to 27 minutes

# AIR FRYER CHICKEN VEGGIE TOT DINNER

*This recipe makes for an easy, delicious, balanced dinner any night of the week. The flavor bursts from the veggies and TJ's amazing 21 Seasoning Salute blend grab your attention from the first bite all the way through that empty plate arrival.*

**2 boneless, skinless chicken breasts, cubed**

**olive oil spray**

**2 teaspoons garlic powder**

**2 teaspoons Italian seasoning**

**1 teaspoon Trader Joe's Spices of the World 21 Seasoning Salute**

**½ pound Trader Joe's Trader Potato Tots, frozen (about ¼ bag)**

**2 bell peppers, chopped**

**4 Roma tomatoes, chopped**

**YIELD: 3 TO 4 SERVINGS**

Preheat the air fryer to 380°F. Put the cubed chicken in a container with a lid. Lightly spray with olive oil, then sprinkle in the seasonings. Cover the container and shake vigorously to coat the chicken with the seasonings.

Place the chunks of chicken in the air fryer basket and cook for 10 minutes. Shake the basket and cook for another 10 minutes. Remove the chicken and set aside. Clean the air fryer basket and lightly spray it with olive oil spray. Reheat the air fryer to 380°F for 3 minutes, then add the potato tots to the basket. Cook for 8 minutes, then shake. Cook for an additional 5 to 7 minutes, until the tots are crisp.

Next, dump in the chicken and veggies with the tots. Use a wooden spoon to mix the ingredients together. Lightly spray with olive oil, then cook for 5 minutes. Remove the chicken-tot blend from the air fryer and serve immediately.

**PREP TIME:** 15 minutes
**COOK TIME:** 41 to 43 minutes
**TOTAL TIME:** 56 to 58 minutes

# THAI-STYLE GREEN CHILI CHICKEN CROSTINI

*I love these for a casual meal that feels kind of elegant. They're easy to make, packed with flavor, and feel a little fancy without all the extra work.*

**1 large boneless, skinless chicken breast**

**6 tablespoons olive oil, divided**

**3 tablespoons Trader Joe's Thai Style Green Chili Sauce, plus more for topping**

**10 slices Trader Joe's Sliced French Brioche**

**2 green bell peppers, cut into rings**

**4 cloves garlic, minced**

**YIELD: 5 SERVINGS**

Place chicken breast, 2 tablespoons olive oil, and Green Chili sauce in a bag or container with a lid. Seal and shake vigorously to blend and coat chicken with the sauce. Put in the fridge and let marinade for 2 hours.

After 2 hours, brush the remaining olive oil over the slices of brioche and place in the air fryer basket. Cook for 5 minutes at 400°F. Flip the bread and cook for another 5 minutes. Bread should be crisp. If it is not, flip and cook again for an additional 3 to 4 minutes.

While the bread is cooking, place the chicken and marinade into a medium skillet. Cook for 10 minutes, then flip the chicken and cook for an additional 5 minutes, or until the chicken is browned and cooked all the way through, reaching an internal temperature of 165°F. Set aside. Plate the bread slices and layer on the sliced bell pepper. Next, cut the chicken into bite-size chunks and top with the minced garlic and a dab of green chili sauce. Serve immediately.

**PREP TIME:** 10 minutes
**REST TIME:** 2 hours
**COOK TIME:** 25 to 29 minutes
**TOTAL TIME:** 2 hour 35 minutes to 2 hours 39 minutes

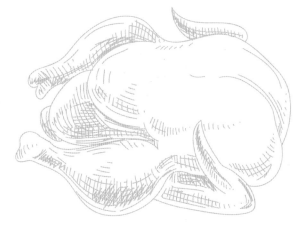

# THAI-STYLE GREEN CHILI CHICKEN NORI WRAPS

*For a twist on the sandwich wrap, I love these nori wraps. They're a bit like sushi while being a bit like a standard salad wrap. They're also completely delicious!*

olive oil spray

2 cups quinoa, cooked

¼ cup rice wine vinegar

1 tablespoon cane sugar

1 large boneless, skinless chicken breast

8 sheets nori

1 large carrot, peeled and shredded

1 cucumber, sliced thin

4 tablespoons Trader Joe's Thai Style Green Chili Sauce

**YIELD: 8 NORI WRAPS**

Spray the air fryer basket with olive oil, then preheat to 350°F. While that's heating up, mix together the cooked quinoa, vinegar, and sugar. Mix together until the quinoa is thoroughly coated and becomes sticky. Lightly spray the chicken breast with olive oil and place it in the air fryer basket. Cook for 10 minutes, flip with tongs, and cook for another 10 minutes, or until the internal temperature reaches 165°F. Once the chicken is done cooking, remove it from the air fryer and let cool for about 15 minutes.

Once the chicken has cooled, lay out 1 nori sheet on a tea towel or sushi roller. Spoon several tablespoons of quinoa into the nori sheet and spread across with a spoon, covering the whole sheet. Using a fork, shred the chicken and place a line of chicken on the inner edge of the nori sheet. Layer in carrots and cucumber, then lightly spread a small amount of the chili sauce over top the veggies.

Carefully roll the contents up, using the tea towel to help. Once the wrap is mostly formed, release the tea towel and finish wrapping. Place the completed wrap seam down on a plate and repeat the process with the rest of the ingredients. Serve immediately.

**PREP TIME:** 30 minutes
**COOK TIME:** 20 minutes
**TOTAL TIME:** 50 minutes

# SHAWARMA CHICKEN THIGHS WITH MOROCCAN RICE

*One of my grandmother's favorite destinations on her round-the-world flight in 1964 was Casablanca in Morocco. While she was visiting the beautiful country, she fell in love with the incredible food. So, my whole life, I have tried her many delectable Moroccan and fusion meals. While this recipe isn't one of hers, it's definitely one she would approve of—and love to make, since it's much faster and easier than most of the ones she used to cook.*

1 cup basmati rice

2 pounds Trader Joe's Shawarma Chicken Thighs

3 tablespoons olive oil

½ large white onion, chopped

1 bay leaf

3 cloves garlic, minced

2 tablespoons Trader Joe's Traditional Harissa

Juice of 1 orange, zest reserved and grated

6 Medjool dates, pitted and diced

**YIELD: 6 SERVINGS**

Prepare rice as usual, being sure to rinse it off thoroughly until the water runs clear before cooking. Once the rice is cooked, preheat the air fryer to 400°F. Put the chicken thighs, with all the marinade, into a pan and cook in the air fryer for 15 minutes. Stir the chicken, pulling up the meat from the bottom of the pan, then cook for another 15 minutes.

While the chicken is cooking, pour the olive oil into a large skillet and heat on medium low. Add the cooked rice and begin stirring. Add the onion and cook for 2 minutes. Stirring constantly, add the bay leaf, garlic, harissa, orange juice and orange zest. Cook for 5 minutes, then add the dates, stirring them in thoroughly. Let the rice mixture cook for 2 to 3 minutes, then remove from the heat.

Plate the chicken and rice together and serve immediately.

**PREP TIME:** 5 minutes
**COOK TIME:** 45 to 55 minutes
**TOTAL TIME:** 55 to 65 minutes

# Chapter 8

# VEGAN-FRIENDLY VICTUALS

# BBQ JACKFRUIT FRIES

*For years I've heard about jackfruit but never really had access to it until moving back to Chicago from a small town in Florida (read: no international groceries and no Trader Joe's!). Then I found the canned jackfruit in brine at TJ's and fell in love.*

*This particular recipe was birthed from my love of Flaco's Tacos' loaded fries. They're nothing like this, but have a similar concept (i.e., loaded). But I wanted something that was vegan-friendly. Thus: these amazing fries that even your meat-eater friends will love.*

**1 (20-ounce) can Trader Joe's Green Jackfruit in Brine**

**1 (24-ounce) package Trader Joe's Handsome Cut Potato Fries, frozen**

**⅓ cup Trader Joe's TJ's Organic Kansas City Style BBQ Sauce**

**¼ white onion, thinly sliced**

**pinch of dried oregano**

**pinch of dried chives**

**YIELD: 4 TO 6 SERVINGS**

Preheat the air fryer to 350°F for 5 minutes. While that's heating up, drain and rinse the jackfruit. Cook in an air fryer pan for 10 minutes, then remove it from the air fryer. Place the fries in the air fryer basket and cook for 15 minutes, shaking the basket every 5 minutes.

While the fries are cooking, shred the jackfruit in the pan, removing any seeds or seed husks. Pour in the BBQ sauce and the onion slices, then thoroughly cover the jackfruit and onions with the sauce. Plate the fries and put the jackfruit in the air fryer to cook with the sauce and onion for 3 minutes. Remove the jackfruit, top the fries with it, and garnish with a pinch of dried oregano and dried chives. Serve immediately.

**PREP TIME:** 5 minutes
**COOK TIME:** 28 minutes
**TOTAL TIME:** 33 minutes

# ASIAN-INSPIRED HEARTS OF PALM STIR-FRY

*For folks looking for a vegan-friendly alternative to the typical stir-fry, this palm noodle option is a delicious and healthy choice. The blend of flavors is incredible and keeps even the meat-eaters happy, thanks to the delectable baked tofu from Trader Joe's.*

1 (7-ounce) package Trader Joe's Organic Baked Tofu Terikayi Flavor

cooking oil spray (soybean, peanut, or coconut)

9 ounces Trader Joe's Hearts of Palm Pasta

2 teaspoons sesame oil

3 tablespoons Trader Joe's Nori Komi Furikake Japanese Multi-Purpose Seasoning

½ cup frozen green peas

¼ large white onion, thinly sliced

4 tablespoons Trader Joe's San Soyaki sauce

**YIELD: 2 TO 3 SERVINGS**

Cut the tofu into squares and spread in your air fryer basket. Make sure the pieces don't overlap. Cook for 5 minutes. Flip the squares and cook for 5 minutes more.

While the tofu is cooking, lightly spray a medium skillet with oil. Heat for 1 minute on medium heat, then add the pasta. Stir the pasta for 1 minute, then add sesame oil. Stir again, coating the pasta lightly with the oil.

Lower the heat to medium-low and add 3 tablespoons of Furikake seasoning. When the tofu is crisp, add it into the mix in the skillet. Add the frozen peas and onion, then pour in the San Soyaki and stir generously, coating everything with the sauce. Let cook, occasionally stirring, for 3 or 4 minutes. When the peas are bright green and slightly soft, the meal is ready to serve.

Dish it out and serve immediately.

**PREP TIME:** 10 minutes
**COOK TIME:** 15 to 17 minutes
**TOTAL TIME:** 25 to 27 minutes

# SRIRACHA TOFU KABOBS WITH JASMINE RICE

*I've always been a big fan of kabobs. We've eaten them in my family since I was pretty small. The most unique experience I ever had with kabobs was noshing on some in the countryside of Russia, near St. Petersburg, where I learned the dish is actually a traditional Georgian meal. My twist on these is vegan friendly and pretty darn tasty, even if I can't spend a few hours this Sunday digging a pit to cook them "properly."*

**2 cups jasmine rice, cooked**

**1 (7-ounce) package Trader Joe's Sriracha Flavored Baked Tofu**

**20 cherry or grape tomatoes**

**20 pearl onions, peeled**

**Asian sweet chili sauce**

**YIELD: 5 OR 6 KABOBS**

Cook your rice before you start the kabobs so they finish around the same time.

Preheat the air fryer to 375°F for 5 minutes. Place the tofu in the air fryer basket and cook for 5 minutes. Remove it from the air fryer and cut the blocks into cubes (approximately 10 per block of tofu). Skewer these chunks along with the tomatoes and onions onto metal or bamboo skewers and place in the basket. Cook for another 5 minutes.

Remove from the air fryer and serve with a side of rice and Asian sweet chili sauce.

**PREP TIME:** 10 minutes
**COOK TIME:** 10 minutes
**TOTAL TIME:** 20 minutes, plus rice cooking time

# JACKFRUIT "CRAB" CAKES

*For those who love the concept of crab cakes but don't eat meat or fish, using jackfruit is an amazing alternative. And TJ's canned jackfruit in brine is the easiest, tastiest way to do all things jackfruit in a snap.*

2 tablespoons ground flaxseed

6 tablespoons water

2 tablespoons Trader Joe's Chile Lime Seasoning Blend

½ teaspoon garlic powder

½ teaspoon sea salt

½ teaspoon ground black pepper

1 teaspoon vegan Worcestershire sauce

2 tablespoons lemon juice

1 (20-ounce) can Trader Joe's Green Jackfruit in Brine, drained and rinsed well, shredded

½ cup regular breadcrumbs

½ cup panko breadcrumbs

lemon wedges, for garnish

vegan tartar sauce or cocktail sauce, for topping

**YIELD: 8 TO 10 CAKES**

Combine the flaxseed and water, mixing thoroughly. Set aside for 10 minutes to thicken. While that's thickening as your "egg," combine all the seasonings, Worcestershire sauce, and lemon juice in a large bowl. Whisk until completely combined.

Next, add the jackfruit and the "egg" and breadcrumbs and combine with your hands until the mixture sticks together.

At this stage, preheat the air fryer to 375°F. Line a baking sheet with parchment paper, then form the jackfruit mixture into patties and place on the baking sheet. Place in the air fryer and cook for 5 to 7 minutes, or until the patties look crisp and golden. Flip and press the lemon juice out of the patties, then cook for another 5 to 7 minutes. Remove and repeat with remaining patties. Serve with lemon wedges, vegan tartar sauce, or cocktail sauce.

**PREP TIME:** 7 to 10 minutes
**REST TIME:** 10 minutes
**COOK TIME:** 10 to 28 minutes
**TOTAL TIME:** 27 to 48 minutes

# SRIRACHA TOFU BURRITOS

*Another fantastic vegan alternative we love in our house is these tofu burritos made from TJ's sriracha tofu. Easy, delicious, and just the right amount of spice.*

**1 (7-ounce) package Trader Joe's Sriracha Flavored Baked Tofu**

**6 large flour tortillas**

**9 ounces black beans, fully cooked**

**½ cup vegan cheese**

**Trader Joe's Chile Lime Seasoning Blend**

**Trader Joe's Pineapple Salsa**

**YIELD: 6 BURRITOS**

Preheat the air fryer to 375°F for 5 minutes. Place the tofu in the air fryer basket and cook for 5 minutes. Using tongs, flip the tofu and cook for another 5 minutes. Remove the blocks from the air fryer, then cut into cubes (approximately 10 per block of tofu).

On plates, set out flour tortillas. Add 3 heaping tablespoons of black beans (fully cooked) into each tortilla. Add several tofu cubes. Spread vegan cheese over the contents, then top with 1 teaspoon chile lime seasoning per burrito.

Wrap together and lay burritos in the air fryer basket, seam down. Cook for 7 minutes. Remove and let stand for 3 minutes, then top with salsa, and serve.

**PREP TIME:** 7 minutes
**COOK TIME:** 17 minutes
**TOTAL TIME:** 24 minutes

# JACKFRUIT TACOS

*Whether you love meat or not, these tacos are delicious, thanks to TJ's fantastically prepared jackfruit and their amazing pico de gallo salsa and BBQ sauce. I mean, seriously. You can't get better than this!*

**1 (20-ounce) can Trader Joe's Green Jackfruit in Brine**

**1 (1.3-ounce) packet Trader Joe's Taco Seasoning Mix**

**¼ cup Trader Joe's Organic Kansas City Style BBQ Sauce**

**8 to 10 taco shells**

**3 cups lettuce, shredded**

**2 large tomatoes, diced**

**½ cup vegan cheese, chopped or shredded**

**½ cup Trader Joe's Mild Pico de Gallo Salsa**

**YIELD: 8 TO 10 TACOS**

Preheat the air fryer to 350°F for 5 minutes. While that's heating up, drain and rinse the jackfruit. Cook for 10 minutes, then remove and place in a small mixing bowl. Shred the jackfruit, removing any seeds or seed husks. Add the taco seasoning and BBQ sauce and cook for an additional 5 minutes.

While the jackfruit is cooking, put your taco shells, lettuce, tomatoes, cheese, pico de gallo, and other goodies out in separate serving dishes so folks can make their tacos how they like. Or, if you prefer service style, set your taco shells up and layer in the lettuce first, tomatoes second, vegan cheese next, and top with jackfruit and a teaspoon of pico de gallo.

**PREP TIME:** 12 minutes
**COOK TIME:** 15 minutes
**TOTAL TIME:** 27 minutes

# VEGGIE BITE ROLLS

*Whatever your penchant, Trader Joe's Organic Veggie Bites are awesome. When you combine them with these other amazing ingredients from TJ's, they become even better. I mean, pepita salsa, tortillas, and vegan cheese? Yeah. These win.*

olive oil spray

1 (12.5-ounce) package Trader Joe's Organic Veggie Bites

4 Trader Joe's Almond Flour Tortillas

4 tablespoons Trader Joe's Pepita Salsa, divided

½ cup vegan cheese, divided

**YIELD: 4 ROLLS**

Preheat the air fryer to 400°F. Lightly spray the air fryer basket with olive oil, then toss in the veggie bites. Cook for 10 minutes or until soft and pliable. Remove from the air fryer and let stand while you prep the wraps.

Plate the tortillas and spread 1 tablespoon of pepita salsa on each tortilla. Next, sprinkle about 2 tablespoons of vegan cheese into each wrap. Now put the veggie bites in, wrap up tightly, flip over, and serve.

**PREP TIME:** 10 minutes
**COOK TIME:** 10 minutes
**TOTAL TIME:** 20 minutes

# SOYAKI JACKFRUIT SUSHI BOWLS

*If you ask me what my favorite meal is, you're almost guaranteed to hear "sushi!" in high, enthusiastic shouts over and over again until you stuff some into my mouth. But I have several friends who are vegan and couldn't enjoy the sushi I usually whip up at home. Knowing the versatility of jackfruit, I thought—why not use that for sushi? The result is this vegan-friendly meal that the whole family can enjoy, fish eaters or not.*

**FOR THE SUSHI RICE**

2 cups white rice

¼ cup rice wine vinegar

¼ cup cane sugar

**FOR THE SUSHI BOWLS**

2 (20-ounce) cans Trader Joe's Green Jackfruit in Brine

4 tablespoons Trader Joe's San Soyaki sauce

2 tablespoons Trader Joe's Nori Komi Furikake Japanese Multi-Purpose Seasoning

4 green onions, chopped fine

1 handful fresh cilantro, stemmed and chopped fine

8 sheets sushi nori

spicy mayo

sushi ginger

**YIELD: 8 BOWLS**

## FOR THE SUSHI RICE

Cook rice as directed on the package (I like to speed things up using my Instant Pot!). When rice is thoroughly cooked and ready, transfer to a large bamboo, wooden, glass, or ceramic bowl (avoid metal). Using a wooden or bamboo spoon, stir in the rice wine vinegar and sugar. Blend thoroughly until rice becomes sticky and aromatic.

## FOR THE SUSHI BOWLS

Preheat the air fryer to 350°F for 5 minutes. While that's heating up, drain and rinse the jackfruit and place in an air fryer pan. Cook for 10 minutes, then remove it and place it in a small mixing bowl. Shred the jackfruit, removing any seeds or seed husks. Pour in the San Soyaki sauce and transfer back into the pan. Cook for another 5 minutes.

Remove the pan and add the seasoning to the dressed jackfruit. Mix thoroughly and set aside.

Line your serving bowls with sheets of nori. Then scoop in approximately 1 cup of sushi rice per bowl. Next, add the San Soyaki jackfruit. Sprinkle green onion and fresh cilantro over the jackfruit. Finally, drizzle on spicy mayo and garnish with ginger. Serve immediately.

**PREP TIME:** 10 minutes
**COOK TIME:** 15 minutes, plus rice cooking time
**TOTAL TIME:** 25 minutes

# BBQ JACKFRUIT STUFFED POTATOES

*These are tasty treats for the whole family—even the meat-eaters. The jackfruit gives the impression of pulled pork with none of the animal product. And if you've ever eaten pulled pork stuffed potatoes, you'll love this healthier alternative for sure.*

4 russet potatoes

olive oil spray

1 (20-ounce) can Trader Joe's Jackfruit in Brine

4 tablespoons Trader Joe's Spicy Cashew Butter Dressing, more for garnish

2 green onions, chopped fine

2 Roma tomatoes, chopped fine

4 slices Trader Joe's Dairy Free Cheddar Style Slices, chopped

**YIELD: 4 STUFFED POTATOES**

Preheat the air fryer to 400°F for 5 minutes. Pierce potatoes, then lightly spray them with olive oil spray on all sides. Place the potatoes in the air fryer basket and cook for 25 minutes. Rotate with tongs and cook for another 20 to 25 minutes.

When the potatoes are nearly done, drain and rinse the jackfruit. Remove the potatoes from the air fryer and set aside. Place the jackfruit into a medium air fryer pan and adjust the temperature down to 350°F. Cook for 10 minutes, then remove and place in a small mixing bowl . Shred the jackfruit, removing any seeds or seed husks. Now pour in the cashew butter dressing and mix thoroughly until the jackfruit is coated. Add in green onions, tomatoes, and cheese. Mix all together.

Now cut your potatoes in half and scoop out about half the contents, setting it aside for another use or disposing of it. Place the potatoes in an air fryer pan. Scoop in the jackfruit mixture and top with a drizzle of the dressing. Cook for 5 minutes. Remove and let stand for 2 to 3 minutes before serving.

**PREP TIME:** 15 minutes
**COOK TIME:** 1 hour to 1 hour 5 minutes
**TOTAL TIME:** 1 hour 15 minutes to 1 hour 20 minutes

# SPICY BUTTERNUT SQUASH FALAFEL

*For a fun alternative to standard falafel, I present spicy butternut squash falafel. Packed with protein and nutrients your body craves, they win in all kinds of ways.*

2 pounds butternut squash

olive oil spray

½ white onion, chopped fine

1 large clove garlic, minced

1½ teaspoons ground cumin

1½ teaspoons ground coriander

1 teaspoon curry powder

⅛ teaspoon cayenne pepper

1 (15-ounce) can Trader Joe's Organic Garbanzo Beans, drained and rinsed

handful fresh cilantro, stemmed

**YIELD: 2 SERVINGS**

Peel and seed the butternut squash and cut into 1-inch cubes. Lightly spray the squash with olive oil, then pop in the air fryer basket. Cook at 350°F for 15 minutes or until the squash is soft. Remove from the air fryer and put the squash in a food processor bowl, along with the remaining ingredients. Process the mixture until the ingredients stick together. (Test with a spoon every so often until the mixture gets there.)

Shape the mixture into 10 to 12 balls and lightly spritz with the olive oil spray again. Put in the air fryer basket and cook again for 10 minutes.

**PREP TIME:** 15 minutes
**COOK TIME:** 25 minutes
**TOTAL TIME:** 40 minutes

# SPICY MAPLE-ROASTED CARROTS

*These are a flavorful side I plan to start serving as a staple for our holiday gatherings, thanks to the warm sweetness of the maple syrup and the zing of the cayenne pepper. They're perfect for any holiday feast—whether Easter, Thanksgiving, or Christmas.*

**1 pound baby-cut carrots**

**½ cup maple syrup**

**1 teaspoon cinnamon**

**½ teaspoon cayenne pepper**

**2 green onions, chopped**

**YIELD: 6 SERVINGS**

Place the carrots, maple syrup, and seasonings in a container with a lid. Cover and shake thoroughly, coating the carrots. Let chill in the fridge for 4 hours to soak in all that maple goodness.

Preheat the air fryer to 350°F. Put the carrots in the air fryer pan, reserving the maple syrup mixture. Cook for 10 minutes. Shake the basket, add the green onions, and cook for another 10 minutes.

Remove the carrots and plate. Drizzle the maple syrup marinade over the carrots and serve immediately.

**PREP TIME:** 5 minutes
**REST TIME:** 4 hours
**COOK TIME:** 20 minutes
**TOTAL TIME:** 4 hours 25 minutes

# BUFFALO TOFU PASTA

*For a fun and delicious twist on all-things-Buffalo, I tossed the sauce with tofu and noodles for this flavor punch. Hopefully you'll enjoy it as much as my guinea pig husband.*

**1 pound rigatoni pasta**

**olive oil spray**

**1 (7-ounce) package Trader Joe's Sriracha Flavored Baked Tofu**

**¼ cup Buffalo wing sauce**

**½ cup Trader Joe's Vegan Caesar Dressing**

**2 stalks celery, chopped**

**1 (3-ounce) package Trader Joe's Sun-Dried Tomatoes, divided**

**YIELD: 4 SERVINGS**

Cook the pasta as directed on packaging. Set aside. Preheat the air fryer to 350°F. Lightly spray the air fryer basket with olive oil and cut the tofu into bite-size cubes. Place the tofu into the basket. Cook for 5 minutes, flip, and cook for another 5 minutes.

While the tofu is cooking, combine the Buffalo sauce and Caesar dressing in a bowl. Plate the pasta and drizzle a small amount of the dressing over the pasta. Place the celery and sun-dried tomatoes on top of the sauce. When the tofu is finished cooking, remove from the air fryer with tongs and evenly spread the tofu across the plates. Drizzle the remaining sauce over the plates, and serve.

**PREP TIME:** 10 minutes
**COOK TIME:** 10 minutes
**TOTAL TIME:** 20 minutes

# EVERYTHING BUT THE BAGEL KALE CHIPS

*For a healthy alternative to potato chips, these kale chips, using TJ's Everything but the Bagel seasoning, are a quick, easy option everybody will love.*

**6 cups packed kale leaves, stems and ribs removed**

**1 tablespoon + 1 teaspoon olive oil**

**2 teaspoons Trader Joe's Everything but the Bagel Seasoning Blend**

**olive oil spray**

**YIELD: 6 SERVINGS**

Preheat the air fryer to 375°F. While that's heating up, wash and completely dry the kale leaves and tear into 2-inch pieces. Toss together the kale, the olive oil and the seasoning. Rub the oil and seasoning into the kale to ensure that it's all covered.

Lightly spray the inside of the air fryer basket. Place the kale inside and cook for 3 minutes. Shake the basket and cook for another 3 minutes. Remove from air fryer and let cool completely before serving.

**PREP TIME:** 10 minutes
**COOK TIME:** 6 minutes
**TOTAL TIME:** 16 minutes

## Chapter 9

# BREAKFAST IS FOR WINNERS

# UBE MOCHI PANCAKES

*Looking for an easy, delicious, gluten-free breakfast that won't take any time at all? Look no further than the unique ube mochi pancakes from Trader Joe's. The delicious mix is made from purple yam and is absolutely to die for!*

**1 (13.3-ounce) box Trader Joe's Ube Mochi Gluten-Free Pancake & Waffle Mix**

**water**

**eggs**

**oil or unsalted butter**

**YIELD: UP TO 6 PANCAKES**

Preheat air fryer to 350° for 5 minutes. While the air fryer is heating up, prepare the pancake batter according to the instructions on the box. Lay a greased, flat pan in the air fryer basket and pour approximately ¼ cup of the batter to create each pancake.

Cook for 4 minutes, then flip and cook for an additional 3 minutes. Repeat as necessary until all pancake batter is used up. Serve with syrup, berries, whipped cream, or whatever your favorite sweet topping is.

**PREP TIME:** 3 to 5 minutes
**COOK TIME:** 7 to 21 minutes
**TOTAL TIME:** 10 to 26 minutes

# TRADER TOT BREAKFAST CASSEROLE

*Breakfast casseroles remain one of my favorite memories of food-related events of childhood. This easy tater tot dish is a delicious offering for a Saturday morning while you watch cartoons with the kids (or on your own!).*

olive oil spray

**3 cups Trader Joe's Trader Potato Tots, frozen**

**¼ cup bacon bits**

**4 green onions, chopped**

**¾ cup shredded cheddar cheese**

**2 tablespoons sour cream**

**YIELD: 6 SERVINGS**

Set the air fryer to 400°F and preheat for 5 minutes. Lightly spray the basket with olive oil, then put in the potato tots. Cook for 5 minutes. Shake the basket and cook for another 5 minutes. Remove the potato tots and put them into a large air fryer pan. Add in the bacon bits and green onions. Top with the cheese.

Reduce heat on the air fryer to 350°F and cook the casserole for 3 minutes, until the cheese melts slightly. Remove it from the air fryer and scoop sour cream over the casserole. Serve immediately.

**PREP TIME:** 5 minutes
**COOK TIME:** 13 minutes
**TOTAL TIME:** 18 minutes

# TRADER TOT EGG CUPS

*Every weekend my hubby and I love to curl up with a hearty breakfast and Saturday morning cartoons. These are the perfect easy meal for the occasion! Protein and carbs to get us going, but easy and fast (once the tots are thawed) so we don't have to wait awhile to eat. And they're absolutely delicious!*

**2½ cups Trader Joe's Trader Potato Tots, thawed**

**4 large eggs**

**1 teaspoon Trader Joe's Chile Lime Seasoning Blend**

**dash of Trader Joe's Everyday Seasoning**

**2 tablespoons shredded cheddar cheese**

**Trader Joe's Pineapple Salsa**

**YIELD: 10 TO 12 CUPS**

In a large mixing bowl, add the thawed potato tots and 1 large egg. Use a potato masher to mash them together, thoroughly coating the potato tots with the egg. Spoon about 1 tablespoon of the mix into silicone baking cups and spread the mix out in the liners, using a spoon. You want the tots to form a solid bottom and sides.

Set the air fryer to 375°F and preheat for 5 minutes. In a separate medium bowl, add 3 eggs, the seasonings, and the shredded cheddar. Mix together thoroughly, breaking the yolks. Spoon the egg mixture into the potato tot cups evenly and cook for 5 to 7 minutes. Top with a teaspoon of pineapple salsa and serve immediately.

**PREP TIME:** 10 minutes
**REST TIME:** 30 to 40 minutes (or overnight in the fridge)
**COOK TIME:** 5 to 7 minutes
**TOTAL TIME:** 45 to 57 minutes

# BACON CAULIFLOWER EGG MUFFINS

*These egg muffins are a great way to pack some fiber, vitamins, and flavor into your morning. I love them for days I'm on the run—they pack neatly into my lunch box and even work as a pick-me-up as I take my morning walk.*

8 eggs

¼ cup unsweetened almond milk

½ cup Trader Joe's Cassava Cauliflower Blend Baking Mix

4 strips bacon, cooked and crumbled

1 green bell pepper, chopped fine

½ cup chopped broccoli

1 teaspoon garlic powder

¼ teaspoon ground black pepper

½ teaspoon dried thyme

1 teaspoon dried chives

olive oil spray

**YIELD: 12 MUFFINS**

Preheat the air fryer to 350°F. In a large bowl, whisk the eggs to break up the yolks and blend together. Add in the milk and whisk again until incorporated. Next, add in the remaining ingredients, except the olive oil. Lightly spray olive oil into 12 silicone baking cups. Fill the cups with the muffin mix, about ¾ full, and place in the air fryer. Cook for 20 minutes. Remove and let stand 3 minutes before serving.

**PREP TIME:** 5 minutes
**COOK TIME:** 20 minutes
**TOTAL TIME:** 25 minutes

# MAPLE PECAN MONKEY BREAD

*The first time I ever had monkey bread was while I was on staff at a summer camp in Georgia. Miss Linda made the bread as a special treat for us teens feeling a little homesick. Now I love making this stuff for gatherings and brunch parties. With TJ's easy puff pastry, it's easier than ever to do.*

½ cup pecans

½ cup cane sugar

1 teaspoon ground cinnamon

½ cup packed brown sugar

¼ cup unsalted butter, room temperature

½ cup water

olive oil spray

2 teaspoons maple syrup

1 (18.3-ounce) package Trader Joe's All Butter Puff Pastry

**YIELD: 6 SERVINGS**

Preheat the air fryer to 350°F. Toss the pecans in the air fryer basket and toast for 6 to 8 minutes. Remove and set aside to cool. While they cool, combine cane sugar and cinnamon in a bowl and set aside. Put the brown sugar, butter, and water into a medium saucepan and bring to a boil over medium heat. Stir until the sugar dissolves and the mixture creates a syrup. Lightly grease an air fryer cake pan with olive oil spray. Pour the syrup into the pan and top with pecans. Add in the maple syrup and set aside.

Roll out the pastry on a lightly floured surface to smooth it out. Stack the two sheets on each other and cut the stack into 48 squares. Roll each square into a ball. Roll the balls in the cinnamon sugar. Put the balls into the cake pan and press down gently into the syrup and pecan topping. Cook for 18 minutes or until golden-brown. Remove from the air fryer and cool slightly before turning upside down and unmolding. Serve warm or cool.

**PREP TIME:** 15 minutes
**COOK TIME:** 24 to 26 minutes
**TOTAL TIME:** 39 to 41 minutes

# PUFF PASTRY APRICOT DANISHES

*I love danishes, but I hate buying store-bought danishes. So, when I realized I could use some of TJ's amazing puff pastry to create my favorite flavors of danish, I was, needless to say, thrilled. Enjoy this simple, easy danish that I make with apricot, but you can use any flavor of TJ's spreads, jams, preserves, or jellies that you like. They're even good with apple butter!*

**8 ounces cream cheese, softened**

**¼ cup cane sugar**

**1 egg**

**1 teaspoon lemon juice**

**1½ teaspoons vanilla extract**

**1 (18.3-ounce) package Trader Joe's All Butter Puff Pastry**

**1 teaspoon water**

**Trader Joe's Organic Apricot Preserves**

**YIELD: 18 SMALL DANISHES**

Combine the cream cheese and sugar in a medium mixing bowl and beat together until smooth. Next, separate the egg yolk and egg white, and add the egg yolk (reserve the egg white), lemon juice, and vanilla, beating until combined. Set aside.

Preheat the air fryer to 400°F. Line baking sheets with parchment paper, then roll out the puff pastry sheets on a clean, dry, flat surface. Cut each sheet into 9 pieces. Prick each piece with a fork several times. Now beat together the reserved egg white and water and brush onto the pastry squares.

At the center of each square, place a dollop of the cream cheese mix, accompanied by 1½ teaspoons of apricot preserves. If desired, fold the edges of the pastry over the filling on two sides. Place the squares on the parchment paper and cook for 10 minutes. Remove from the air fryer and let cool on drying racks before serving.

**PREP TIME:** 10 minutes
**COOK TIME:** 10 minutes
**TOTAL TIME:** 20 minutes

# CRISPY FRENCH TOAST STICKS

*Who doesn't love French toast? And who wouldn't love a fun way to eat them? These crispy French toast sticks do just that—turning them from fork-cutting goodness into dipping deliciousness.*

**5 slices Trader Joe's Whole Wheat Bread**

**2 eggs**

**⅓ cup milk**

**2 tablespoons flour**

**3 tablespoons cane sugar**

**1 teaspoon vanilla extract**

**2 teaspoons ground cinnamon**

**confectioners' sugar for dusting (optional)**

**maple syrup for dipping (optional)**

**YIELD: 15 STICKS**

Preheat the air fryer to 370°F. While that's heating up, cut each slice of bread into 3 pieces and set aside. Combine the eggs, milk, flour, sugar, vanilla, and cinnamon in a shallow bowl, whisking to combine. Dip each stick of bread into the mix, coating both sides and ends. Lay a piece of parchment paper in the air fryer basket, then put French toast sticks onto the parchment paper.

Cook the toast sticks for 5 minutes, then with tongs flip them over and cook for an additional 5 minutes. Remove the toast sticks from the air fryer. Dust with confectioners' sugar and serve immediately dusted with confectioners' sugar or with maple syrup for dipping, if using.

**PREP TIME:** 10 minutes
**COOK TIME:** 10 minutes
**TOTAL TIME:** 20 minutes

# PUFF PASTRY APPLE BREAKFAST SANDWICHES

*A fun, easy way to make breakfast extra special is with these decadently sweet apple pastry sandwiches. They're perfect for packing off with the kids as they head out to play or for just casual noshing on goodness while you drink a cup of coffee first thing.*

1 (8-ounce) package cream cheese, softened

¼ cup cane sugar

½ teaspoon vanilla extract

2 large egg yolks, divided

2 tablespoons water

1 (18.3-ounce) package Trader Joe's All Butter Puff Pastry

1 Gala or Fuji apple, thinly sliced

olive oil spray

**YIELD: 4 SANDWICHES**

Preheat the air fryer to 325°F. While it's heating up, beat together the cream cheese, sugar, and vanilla until smooth. Add in 1 egg yolk and beat again until smooth.

Mix the water and other egg yolk together with a fork. Then, on a lightly floured surface, unroll the sheets of pastry dough. Cut the dough into 4 squares each. Spoon the cream cheese mix into the centers of half the squares, then top each square with 4 to 6 slices of apple. Brush the other pastry dough squares with the egg-and-water mix, then place the square on top of those with the cream cheese and apples. Press the edges together.

Lightly spray a baking sheet or line with parchment paper, then place the apple sandwiches on the tray. Place in the air fryer and cook for 8 to 10 minutes or until golden-brown. When done, remove and let stand for 5 minutes before serving.

**PREP TIME:** 10 minutes
**COOK TIME:** 8 to 10 minutes
**TOTAL TIME:** 18 to 20 minutes

# SOFFRITTO BREAKFAST POTATO WEDGES

*Sometimes I like a spicy kick to wake up the day. These soffritto potato wedges are the perfect way to do that. They also make a great side with the egg muffins for a fuller breakfast.*

**4 russet potatoes, cut into wedges**

**olive oil spray**

**2 teaspoons Trader Joe's Italian Style Soffritto Seasoning Blend**

**1 teaspoon garlic powder**

**1 teaspoon smoked paprika**

**2 green onions, chopped**

**sour cream**

**YIELD: 6 SERVINGS**

Preheat the air fryer to 400°F. Put the potato wedges in a plastic container with a lid, and lightly spray with olive oil. Add the seasonings, cover the container, and shake vigorously to coat the wedges.

Place the wedges, along with the green onions, in the air fryer basket. Cook for 15 minutes, shaking the basket every 5 minutes. If the potatoes aren't as crisp as you like, cook for an additional 5 minutes. Remove the potatoes and let stand for 3 minutes before plating and topping with a dollop of sour cream per serving.

**PREP TIME:** 3 minutes
**COOK TIME:** 15 to 20 minutes
**TOTAL TIME:** 18 to 23 minutes

# NUTTY AIR FRYER GRANOLA

*I'm a huge granola fan—have been my whole life, thanks to an amazing family recipe. Of course, our family recipe is made in the oven and is more loaded with calories than I'd like to think about. This one's a little less calorie dense and so much easier and faster to make, thanks to our wonderful friend the air fryer. Enjoy!*

**2 cups rolled oats**

**½ cup toasted wheat germ**

**½ cup Trader Joe's Freeze Dried Blueberries or Strawberries**

**½ cup dried cherries**

**⅛ cup pepitas**

**¼ cup Trader Joe's Roasted & Unsalted Sunflower Seeds**

**1 tablespoon flaxseed**

**¼ cup chopped pecans**

**½ cup Trader Joe's Nuts Raw California Premium Walnut Halves, chopped**

**¼ cup Trader Joe's Nuts Raw Sliced Almonds**

**1 teaspoon ground cinnamon**

**2 tablespoons Trader Joe's Raw & Unfiltered Hawaiian Macadamia Nut Blossom & Multi-Floral Honey**

**1 teaspoon vanilla extract**

**¼ cup maple syrup**

**6 tablespoons coconut oil**

**YIELD: 8 TO 10 SERVINGS**

Preheat the air fryer to 350°F. While that's warming up, combine all the dry ingredients in a large mixing bowl. Then add in the honey, vanilla extract, maple syrup, and coconut oil, stirring together until everything is fully coated. Pour the contents into an air fryer pan and cook for 15 minutes, stirring the contents every 5 minutes. Remove from the air fryer and allow the granola to cool completely before serving.

**PREP TIME:** 5 minutes
**COOK TIME:** 15 minutes
**TOTAL TIME:** 20 minutes

# HOMEMADE "POP TARTS"

*For a tasty homemade treat with Trader Joe's amazing preserves, these decadent and super-easy "pop tarts" have the win. And they take just a few minutes to prep and cook.*

### FOR THE "POP TARTS"

1 (22-ounce) package Trader Joe's Pie Crusts, thawed

8 tablespoons Trader Joe's Organic Strawberry Preserves Reduced Sugar

water

olive oil spray

### FOR THE ICING

2¼ cups powdered sugar

4 tablespoons heavy cream

2 tablespoons melted unsalted butter

1½ teaspoons vanilla extract

sprinkles (optional)

**YIELD: 8 POP TARTS**

Lay out the pie crusts flat on a baking sheet. Using a pizza cutter, cut each crust into 4 equally sized squares. Combine the extra dough and roll out again and cut into 4 squares again each. You will have 16 squares total.

Place 1 tablespoon of preserves on half the squares. Spread with a spoon, leaving about ¼ inch around the edges.

Preheat the air fryer to 350°F. Now dip your fingers into clean water and moisten the edge of the outside of each piece of dough. Then top the preserves-filled squares with the other dough pieces. Use your fingers to pinch the seams together. Use a fork to crimp the edges, then use a knife to poke tiny holes or slits into the top of each tart.

Lightly spray the air fryer basket with olive oil spray, then place the tarts into the basket. Cook for 10 to 12 minutes, or until the dough crisps and turns golden-brown. Remove and let cool completely before topping with icing.

To make the icing, whisk together the powdered sugar, heavy cream, butter, and vanilla extract in a small bowl until well combined. When the tarts are completely cooled, spread a bit on each tart and top with sprinkles, if using. Pop into the fridge and let chill for 1 hour before serving.

**PREP TIME:** 10 minutes
**COOK TIME:** 10 to 12 minutes
**TOTAL TIME:** 20 to 22 minutes

# FIG BANANA BREAD WITH WALNUTS

*If you ask anyone who's tried my baked goods, you'll hear that I'm 100% all about fruit breads. I adore making banana bread, strawberry bread, blueberry bread, raspberry bread... If it's fruit, it belongs in bread, in my opinion. And this just happens to be my go-to fruit bread recipe with some tweaks. I mean, figs and bananas? Absolutely amazingly delicious!*

**2 overripe bananas, mashed**

**½ cup Trader Joe's Fig Butter**

**1 teaspoon baking soda**

**⅓ cup unsalted butter, melted**

**¾ cup cane sugar**

**pinch salt**

**2 large eggs, beaten**

**1 teaspoon vanilla extract**

**1½ cups all-purpose flour**

**½ cup walnuts, chopped**

**YIELD: 6 SERVINGS**

Preheat the air fryer to 350°F. Grease a 4 x 8-inch loaf pan (or an equivalent that works in your air fryer). In a medium mixing bowl, combine the mashed bananas and fig butter. Mix together until smooth. Mix in the baking soda, then stir in the melted butter. Now add the sugar, salt, eggs, and vanilla. Mix thoroughly. Then add in the flour, a ½ cup at a time. Finally, stir in the walnuts and blend until incorporated.

Pour the batter into the pan and cook for 25 to 30 minutes. Check with a toothpick. If it comes out clean, the bread is ready. If not, continue cooking in 5-minute intervals until ready. Remove the pan from the air fryer and let stand for 10 minutes. Flip the pan to remove the bread and cool completely on a drying rack before cutting and serving.

**PREP TIME:** 10 minutes
**COOK TIME:** 25 to 30 minutes
**TOTAL TIME:** 35 to 40 minutes

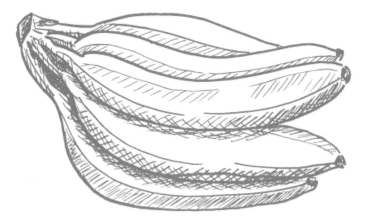

# CHILE LIME FRITTATAS

*Frittatas are an amazing way to basically enjoy a giant, easy omelet. I love blending together eggs, veggies, and seasonings to create that perfect breakfast meal, so I decided to give it a go with my favorite TJ's spice blend: Chile Lime.*

**6 ounces Trader Joe's Sweet Italian Style Chicken Sausage, diced (approximately half the package)**

**4 large eggs, lightly beaten**

**½ cup shredded mozzarella cheese**

**¼ red bell pepper, diced**

**2 green onions, chopped**

**1 teaspoon Trader Joe's Chile Lime Seasoning Blend**

**olive oil spray**

**YIELD: 2 SERVINGS**

Preheat the air fryer to 360°F. Combine all the ingredients, except the olive oil spray, in a medium bowl and mix together. Spray an air fryer cake pan with olive oil spray, then pour the egg mixture into the pan. Cook for 18 to 20 minutes. Remove from the air fryer, let stand for 5 minutes, and serve.

**PREP TIME:** 3 minutes
**COOK TIME:** 18 to 20 minutes
**TOTAL TIME:** 21 to 23 minutes

# GLUTEN-FREE BREAKFAST BURRITO

*I love breakfast burritos. Seriously. So a-ma-zingly delicious! But being gluten-free, I usually can't eat them. Well, with the help of TJ's cauliflower thins, I've fixed that problem. And man, are they delicious!*

**2 large eggs**

**1 teaspoon taco seasoning**

**1 (4.5-ounce) package Trader Joe's Cauliflower Thins**

**Trader Joe's Mild Pico de Gallo Salsa, more for garnish**

**4 tablespoons shredded cheddar cheese, divided**

**2 teaspoons chile peppers, chopped fine, divided**

**hot sauce (optional)**

**YIELD: 4 BURRITOS**

Scramble the eggs with taco seasoning and set aside. Preheat the air fryer to 400°F. While that's heating up, place each cauliflower thin on a small sheet of aluminum foil large enough to wrap around the burritos completely. Layer in pico de gallo, cheese, and chiles, then top with the egg. Wrap the thins like a burrito, then fold the foil up around them.

Place the foil-wrapped burritos in the air fryer basket and cook for 10 minutes. Remove and let cool for 5 minutes, then serve with a little extra pico de gallo or hot sauce, if using.

**PREP TIME:** 7 minutes
**COOK TIME:** 10 minutes
**TOTAL TIME:** 17 minutes

# Chapter 10

# GLUTEN-FREE GOODNESS

# GLUTEN-FREE SAUSAGE FETA PIZZA

*One of my biggest complaints about having to live a gluten-free lifestyle (thank you, food allergies!) is that there's so little pizza out there worth eating. Well, thanks to TJ's, that problem is solved. These easy personal pizzas are delicious and fast. Even I can't complain!*

**2 Trader Joe's Cauliflower Pizza Crusts**

**4 tablespoons Trader Giotto's Fat Free Pizza Sauce**

**1 link Trader Joe's Garlic Herb Chicken Sausage**

**1 ounce Trader Joe's Crumbled Feta (approximately ⅙ of a container)**

**handful fresh cilantro**

**2 servings Trader Joe's Sun-Dried Tomatoes**

**olive oil spray**

**YIELD: 2 INDIVIDUAL PIZZAS**

Preheat the air fryer to 350°F for 5 minutes. Lay the crusts out flat on a plate or clean surface. Spoon 2 tablespoons of pizza sauce over each crust. Next, chop up the sausage into small bite-size pieces and lay out over both pizzas. Then sprinkle feta over the pizzas, followed by the cilantro and sun-dried tomatoes.

Gently spray the basket with olive oil and put each pizza in the air fryer, laying them out flat. If your air fryer is too small for this, gently fold the pizza in half, shifting the toppings to one side to accommodate. Cook for 5 minutes, then remove and cook the second pizza. Let stand for 5 minutes, then serve.

........................................................

For a crisper crust, gently brush egg whites on both sides of the crusts before topping and cooking.

........................................................

**PREP TIME:** 5 minutes
**COOK TIME:** 5 to 10 minutes
**REST TIME:** 5 minutes
**TOTAL TIME:** 15 to 20 minutes

# EVERYTHING BUT THE ELOTE CHORIZO CANAPES

*I absolutely adore anything cauliflower. Whoever thought of turning it into crusts and bread alternatives is seriously a genius. And TJ's is genius for making these cauliflower thins en masse for us gluten-free folks who just don't have the energy to make them ourselves. Now enjoy the celebration with me by whipping up a batch of these oh-so-flavorful canapes for a snack or your next party.*

**4 ounces Trader Joe's Soy Chorizo**

**4 Trader Joe's Cauliflower Thins**

**4 tablespoons tomato sauce**

**8 tablespoons shredded cheddar cheese**

**2 teaspoons Trader Joe's Everything but the Elote Seasoning Blend**

**YIELD: 4 CANAPES**

Lightly spray the air fryer basket and preheat the air fryer to 350°F for 5 minutes. Prick tiny holes in the chorizo and place in the basket. Cook for 7 to 9 minutes. Remove from the basket and slit open and break into crumbles.

On a plate, lay out the cauliflower thins, making sure they are flat. In a bowl, combine the tomato sauce, chorizo crumbles, cheese, and seasoning blend. Mix together, then spoon approximately a quarter over each cauliflower thin.

Lay the cauliflower "canapes" flat in the air fryer basket and cook for 3 to 5 minutes. Remove and let stand for 2 minutes before serving.

**PREP TIME:** 3 to 5 minutes
**COOK TIME:** 10 to 14 minutes
**TOTAL TIME:** 13 to 19 minutes

# ZESTY CAULIFLOWER GNOCCHI

*Being gluten-free, I'm always on the lookout for incredible, easy, and delicious foods from TJ's for dinner. When I spotted the cauliflower gnocchi, I knew I'd found a winner—gnocchi is one of my absolute faves! Toss in a little spicy soffritto—and bam! Easy, fast, and a little kicky to satisfy all those points.*

**12 ounces Trader Joe's Cauliflower Gnocchi**

**olive oil spray**

**1 tablespoon Trader Joe's Italian Style Soffritto Seasoning Blend**

**1 cup Trader Giotto's Traditional Marinara Sauce**

**YIELD: 2 TO 3 SERVINGS**

Preheat the air fryer to 400°F for 5 minutes. While that's warming up, put the gnocchi in a container with a lid and lightly coat with olive oil spray. Sprinkle in the seasoning blend. Cover and shake thoroughly to coat gnocchi in seasoning and oil.

Cook in the air fryer for 5 minutes. Toss the gnocchi in the basket and cook for another 5 minutes. Serve with traditional marinara or another favorite sauce.

Hint: For extra-crispy gnocchi, cook for a total of 15 minutes, tossing in the basket every 5 minutes.

**PREP TIME:** 2 minutes
**COOK TIME:** 10 minutes
**TOTAL TIME:** 12 minutes

# CHEESY ITALIAN TRADER TOT CASSEROLE

*This one has become one of my new favorites. Admittedly, it's not what you'd call healthy—for some just delicious comfort food—this is an easy, fast winner every time.*

**2 cups Trader Joe's Trader Potato Tots**

**48 slices turkey pepperoni (approximately 3 servings)**

**1 cup canned diced tomatoes**

**1½ cups shredded cheddar cheese**

**1 teaspoon dried rosemary**

**½ teaspoon dried thyme**

**2 teaspoons garlic powder**

**¼ teaspoon black pepper**

**1 teaspoon paprika**

**2 teaspoons Italian seasoning**

**YIELD: 3 TO 4 SERVINGS**

In a medium bowl, combine the diced tomatoes, cheese, and seasonings. Mix well, combining them as thoroughly as possible. Next, place the pepperoni in an air fryer pan, then add the potato tots to the pan. Layer the tomato-and-cheese mixture on top. Cook at 400°F for 5 minutes. Remove the pan, stir lightly to get the cheese exposed thoroughly, then cook for an additional 3 to 5 minutes.

Remove from the air fryer, stir all ingredients together thoroughly, then let stand for 1 to 2 minutes. Serve and enjoy!

**PREP TIME:** 5 minutes
**COOK TIME:** 8 to 10 minutes
**TOTAL TIME:** 13 to 15 minutes

# LOADED GREEK FRIES WITH FETA AND TOMATO

*To be honest, I wouldn't have thought of doing Greek-themed fries if it weren't for my husband's intense love of olives and feta cheese. In exploring some ideas for quick, easy meals, I pulled the ingredients out of the fridge and tossed these together. And even though I'm not a fan of olives, these are still pretty darn tasty.*

olive oil spray

**12 ounces Trader Joe's Handsome Cut Fries (approximately half the bag)**

**4 Roma tomatoes, sliced**

**¼ cup black olives, slices**

**¼ cup Trader Joe's Authentic Greek Feta**

**¼ cup Trader Joe's Tzatziki Creamy Garlic Cucumber Dip**

**YIELD: 5 TO 6 SERVINGS**

Preheat the air fryer to 350°F. Lightly spray the air fryer basket and toss the fries in. Cook for 15 minutes, shaking the basket every 5 minutes. Plate the fries and carefully layer on the tomatoes, olives, and feta, then pour the sauce over the fries. Serve immediately.

**PREP TIME:** 5 minutes
**COOK TIME:** 15 minutes
**TOTAL TIME:** 20 minutes

# GLUTEN-FREE CABERNET BEEF JOHNNY MARZETTI

*So, I'm not entirely sure where my family got the name "Johnny Marzetti" for this dish that's vaguely similar to goulash, but it's the name I always grew up with. In this particular recipe, I tweaked the "toss a bit of this, a bit of that into the pot" concept and used the amazing Trader Joe's Cabernet Beef Pot Roast instead of our family's traditional ground chuck. Enjoy!*

**1 pound gluten-free elbow macaroni**

**approximately 1 pound Trader Joe's Cabernet Beef Pot Roast,**

**1 (28-ounce) can diced tomatoes**

**2 tablespoons red wine vinegar**

**1¼ teaspoons Trader Joe's Chile Lime Seasoning Blend**

**2 teaspoons garlic powder**

**2 teaspoons dried oregano**

**2 teaspoons dried thyme**

**¼ teaspoon ground black pepper**

**4 cups fresh spinach**

**1 yellow onion, chopped**

**2 cups shredded cheddar cheese**

**YIELD: 4 TO 5 SERVINGS**

Preheat your air fryer to 350°F for 5 minutes. While that's heating up, cube your beef. Place the chunks of beef into the basket of your air fryer and cook for 10 minutes. Using tongs, flip the chunks of beef and cook for another 10 minutes. The meat should be a little pink in the middle when you remove it from the air fryer.

While the meat is cooking, in a large saucepan, prepare your gluten-free macaroni as the directions on the package recommend. Remove the pasta from the pan, drain, and rinse (most packages will say not to rinse, but I hate that weird texture left afterward if I don't rinse), then return the pasta to the pan. Add in the diced tomatoes, red wine vinegar, and seasonings, and put on medium-low heat. When the meat is ready, add it to the pot and stir it in. Cook for 5 minutes, then add in the spinach, onion, and cheddar. Cook for another 5 minutes or until the cheese is melted and stringy. Remove from heat, let stand for 2 to 3 minutes, then serve.

**PREP TIME:** 5 minutes
**COOK TIME:** 30 minutes
**TOTAL TIME:** 35 minutes

# SOY CHORIZO BUNS

*I think most of us can say we love pastry. From the sweet, flaky danishes to the savory, rich dinner rolls—pastry wins. I also happen to love Trader Joe's soy chorizo, so combining the two seemed like the perfect choice for a glorious meal. I was not wrong!*

1 cup warm water

3 tablespoons cane sugar

1 package dry yeast (approximately 2¼ teaspoons)

3¼ cups gluten-free all-purpose flour

3 tablespoons olive oil

¼ teaspoon salt

olive oil spray

1 (12-ounce) package Trader Joe's Soy Chorizo

1½ teaspoons baking powder

3 green onions, chopped fine

**YIELD: 10 TO 12 BUNS**

Combine the water, sugar, and yeast in a large mixing bowl, mixing thoroughly. Cover and let stand for 5 minutes for the yeast to properly activate.

Once the yeast is activated (the mixture will become bubbly or frothy looking), slowly add flour, oil, and salt to the yeast mixture. Stir together until a dough forms. Set aside. Sprinkle a clean, flat, dry surface with gluten-free flour. Remove dough from bowl and place it on the floured surface. Knead the dough until it is smooth and elastic, about 10 minutes. Lightly spray the inside of a large mixing bowl and place the dough in to rise. Cover the bowl and let rise for 1 hour, or until the dough has doubled in size.

Punch the dough down, then let it rest for 5 minutes.

While the dough is standing, lightly spray the air fryer basket with olive oil, then preheat the air fryer to 350°F for 5 minutes. Prick tiny holes in the chorizo casing and place in the basket. Cook for 7 to 9 minutes.

While the chorizo is cooking, return the dough to a clean, dry surface and knead in the baking powder. Let the dough rest for an additional 5 minutes.

Remove the chorizo, then slit open the casing and pour the contents into a small mixing bowl. Add the chopped green onion and combine. Set aside.

Now divide the dough into 10 to 12 equal portions. Using your hands, shape the dough into balls and set it aside. Take a ball and roll with a floured rolling pin until a disk about ¼-inch thick forms. Spoon the chorizo/onion mix into the disks, leaving enough dough at the edges to fold up around the filling. Fold the edges up, bringing them to the center. Pinch together at the center, then set aside. Repeat the process with all the dough balls.

Spray more olive oil in the air fryer basket, then place the chorizo buns inside. Lightly spray the tops of the buns and cook for 7 to 10 minutes, or until golden-brown on top. Remove the buns from the air fryer and let stand for 5 minutes before serving.

**PREP TIME:** 30 minutes
**COOK TIME:** 14 to 19 minutes
**REST TIME:** 1 hour 10 minutes
**TOTAL TIME:** 1 hour 24 minutes to 1 hour 29 minutes

# EASY, FAST CABERNET BEEF SHEPHERD'S PIE

*Okay, okay, so meat drenched in wine isn't exactly a "poor man's" meal, as the "shepherd's pie" title implies. But, well, I just love this marinade and wanted to give it a shot as the meat base for one of my favorite meals. It absolutely does not disappoint and certainly elevates the level of this traditionally "cheap" meal with only a little bit higher price tag.*

**approximately 1 pound Trader Joe's Cabernet Beef Pot Roast**

**1 pound Trader Joe's Mashed Cauliflower, frozen**

**2 cups frozen vegetables (peas, green beans, carrots, broccoli, or stir-fry veggies are all great choices)**

**1 teaspoon salt**

**½ teaspoon ground black pepper**

**2 teaspoons dried thyme**

**2 teaspoons dried rosemary**

**1 tablespoon garlic powder**

**1 teaspoon dried parsley**

**1 small yellow onion, chopped**

**YIELD: 6 TO 8 SERVINGS**

Preheat the air fryer to 350°F for 5 minutes. While that's heating up, chop the raw beef into bite-size chunks. When the air fryer is ready, put the meat into the basket as is, and cook for 10 minutes. Using tongs, flip the meat after the initial cook time, then cook for another 10 minutes.

While the meat is cooking, prepare the mashed cauliflower as the package directs. You'll also want to use this time to place the frozen veggies into a steamer and steam for approximately 15 minutes to get the veggies fully soft and moist.

If the meat isn't fully cooked at this point, you can turn the pieces a second time and cook for an additional 5 to 7 minutes to get it fully done. If you prefer the meat a little rarer, it should be good to go as is.

Once all the components of the meal are finished, dump all the ingredients into a large pot or serving bowl together and stir thoroughly, to incorporate completely. Serve hot.

**PREP TIME:** 5 minutes
**COOK TIME:** 20 minutes
**TOTAL TIME:** 25 minutes

# MAC 'N CHEESE CASSEROLE

*There's nothing quite like a good mac 'n cheese. Make it gluten-free and add bacon bits, onions, and seasonings and you just might have the perfect meal for this gal!*

1 (12-ounce) package Trader Joe's Gluten Free Mac & Cheese, frozen

2 tablespoons bacon bits, additional for garnish

3 green onions, chopped

½ cup white onion, chopped

2 teaspoons garlic powder

2 teaspoons dried chives

¼ teaspoon ground black pepper

½ cup gluten-free breadcrumbs

chopped fresh cilantro, for garnish (optional)

**YIELD: 2 SERVINGS**

Preheat your air fryer to 375°F. Remove the outer package and film wrap from the mac & cheese. Place on a baking sheet and cook in the air fryer for 10 minutes. Stir and cook for another 10 minutes. When the mac & cheese is ready, pour it into a pan for the air fryer. Mix in the bacon bits, green onions, white onion, and seasonings. Spread the breadcrumbs over top and put in the air fryer.

Cook for 10 minutes, then remove and let stand for 5 minutes. Garnish with additional bacon bits and fresh cilantro, if using, and serve hot.

**PREP TIME:** 5 minutes
**COOK TIME:** 30 minutes
**TOTAL TIME:** 35 minutes

# MEXICAN-STYLE CORN ON THE COB

*Street food is always the best way to go (if you can do so safely!) while traveling. Of course, when you're not traveling, it's nice to bring some of those options home. With an air fryer, these foods are easier than ever to make, from Mexican-style corn to the plantain chips and more.*

**2 tablespoons unsalted butter, melted**

**4 ears of corn, shucked**

**2 teaspoons Trader Joe's Chile Lime Seasoning Blend**

**⅓ cup sour cream**

**¼ cup chopped fresh cilantro**

**¼ teaspoon salt**

**¼ teaspoon ground black pepper**

**½ cup Mexican-style shredded cheese**

**YIELD: 4 EARS OF CORN**

Preheat the air fryer to 400°F. Brush about ½ a teaspoon of butter onto each ear of corn, coating all sides. Reserve the leftover butter for the sauce. Put the corn in the air fryer basket and cook for 5 minutes, then, using tongs, turn the cobs and cook for another 5 minutes. While the corn is cooking, combine the other ingredients, except the cheese, in a medium shallow bowl to make a sauce.

Remove the corn from the air fryer and baste with the sauce. Sprinkle the cheese over the corn and return it to the air fryer basket. Cook for 2 to 3 minutes until the cheese melts slightly. Remove and let stand for 2 to 3 minutes before serving.

**PREP TIME:** 7 minutes
**COOK TIME:** 10 minutes
**TOTAL TIME:** 17 minutes

# COCONUT ALMOND CHICKEN STRIPS

*Another pet peeve of mine as a gluten-free gal is the sheer lack of tasty chicken nuggets I can nosh on for an easy dinner choice. Well, thanks to TJ's amazing seasoning blends and almond flour, that problem is solved.*

**1 pound boneless, skinless chicken breast, cut into strips**

**2 large eggs**

**1 cup Trader Joe's Blanched Almond Flour**

**1 teaspoon garlic powder**

**¼ teaspoon ground black pepper**

**1 teaspoon Trader Joe's Spices of the World 21 Seasoning Salute**

**¼ teaspoon baking powder**

**olive oil spray**

**dipping sauce of choice**

**YIELD: 2 TO 3 SERVINGS**

Preheat the air fryer to 400°F. Rinse off the chicken strips and pat dry with a paper towel. Set aside. In a shallow bowl, beat the eggs. In a second shallow bowl, combine the almond flour, spices, and baking powder.

Spray the air fryer basket with olive oil spray. Dip each chicken strip first into the egg wash, then into the flour mixture, then gently place each strip in the air fryer basket in a single layer. Spray the chicken strips with olive oil, then cook for 7 minutes. Carefully flip them over with tongs, then cook for another 7 minutes. Repeat with the remaining chicken strips.

Remove the chicken strips from the air fryer and let stand for 3 minutes before serving with your favorite dipping sauce.

**PREP TIME:** 12 minutes
**COOK TIME:** 28 minutes
**TOTAL TIME:** 40 minutes

# GENERAL TSAO'S CAULIFLOWER WITH RICE NOODLES

*The problem with most Chinese restaurants is there's almost nothing gluten-free on the buffets. I've missed having General Tsao's anything (as well as sesame chicken, orange chicken, etc., etc.!), but with TJ's sauce and some tasty cauliflower, I can resolve that issue in a healthy way.*

½ **large head of cauliflower, chopped into bite-size pieces**

½ **tablespoon sesame oil**

1 **teaspoon garlic powder**

½ **cup Trader Ming's General Tsao Stir Fry Sauce**

**uncooked rice noodles to make 2 cups**

4 **green onions, chopped**

**YIELD: 4 SERVINGS**

In a container with a lid, toss together the cauliflower, sesame oil, garlic powder and General Tsao sauce, completely coating the cauliflower. Cover the container and let the cauliflower absorb the sauce for 4 hours.

When the 4 hours are up, prepare rice noodles as directed on the package. While that's cooking, preheat your air fryer to 400°F. Pull out the cauliflower and pour into an air fryer pan with all the sauce. Cook for 10 minutes, stir around a bit, then cook for another 10 minutes.

When the cauliflower is done, remove from the air fryer and let stand while you plate the noodles. Add the green onions to the pan and mix in with the cauliflower. Then top the noodles with the cauliflower mix, drizzling some of the sauce over the noodles. Serve immediately.

**PREP TIME:** 7 to 10 minutes
**REST TIME:** 4 hours
**COOK TIME:** 10 minutes
**TOTAL TIME:** 4 hours, 17 to 20 minutes

# Chapter 11

# SHOW ME THE SANDWICH

# CHICAGO-STYLE CABERNET ITALIAN BEEF SANDWICHES

*Living in Chicago, I've learned to appreciate some new sandwich types I never would have considered before. The Chicago-style Italian beef, for example. My friend Jeff introduced me to them at the famous Al's Beef downtown. Unfortunately, they don't have any gluten-free choices. But making them at home now, I can use gluten-free hoagies for myself and enjoy the wonders!*

**approximately 2 pounds Trader Joe's Cabernet Beef Pot Roast**

**1 tablespoon olive oil**

**1 medium white onion, thinly sliced**

**1 teaspoon sea salt**

**½ teaspoon ground black pepper**

**1 tablespoon Italian seasoning**

**2 teaspoons dried thyme**

**1½ teaspoons crushed red pepper**

**½ cup red wine**

**2 cups beef stock**

**4 green bell peppers, thinly sliced**

**6 cloves garlic, minced**

**4 gluten-free hoagie rolls**

**giardiniera, for topping**

**YIELD: 4 SANDWICHES**

Preheat the air fryer to 350°F for 5 minutes. While the air fryer heats up, cut the beef in half. Place the beef in the air fryer basket and cook for 10 minutes. Flip the meat pieces and expose the underside, then cook for 10 minutes more.

While the meat is cooking, in a medium skillet on medium heat, heat 1 tablespoon of olive oil. Next, put the onions and seasonings in the pan and stir into the oil for 2 minutes. Add the red wine and thoroughly incorporate the seasonings. Reduce the heat by half and cook for 3 minutes. Add the beef stock and bring to a simmer.

When the beef is cooked, add it to the pan simmering on the stove and cook for 5 minutes. Add the bell peppers and garlic to the pan, stirring constantly. Cook until the peppers are soft, 3 to 5 minutes.

Turn off the heat and remove the meat, peppers, and onions from the pan, reserving the sauce in the pan.

Plate your hoagie rolls and cut evenly lengthwise. Slice the meat thinly and layer it into the rolls with the pepper and onions. Drizzle a tablespoon of the sauce over the meat, then add in giardiniera. Keep the remaining sauce in a small bowl for dipping, and serve.

**PREP TIME:** 5 to 7 minutes
**COOK TIME:** 28 to 30 minutes
**TOTAL TIME:** 33 to 37 minutes

# GLUTEN-FREE BEEFY SANDWICHES WITH PEPPER JELLY

*This simple, delicious sandwich won me over the second I spotted the pepper jelly in the fridge. Instantly, I knew the cab beef from TJ's and the jelly would be perfect together—and let me tell you, they are!*

**1 pound Trader Joe's Cabernet Beef Pot Roast**

**8 slices wheat bread**

**Trader Joe's Hot & Sweet Pepper Jelly**

**lettuce**

**YIELD: 4 LARGE SANDWICHES**

Preheat the air fryer to 350°F for 5 minutes. Cut the beef in half and then pour the beef and liquid contents into a medium air fryer pan and cook for 10 minutes. With tongs, flip the beef to expose the undercooked side. Cook for another 10 minutes. Flip the meat again and cook for 5 to 10 minutes, depending on how well done you like your meat.

During the last phase of cooking, toast your wheat bread and plate. Spread on the pepper jelly and add some lettuce.

When the meat is finished cooking, let stand for 5 minutes, then thinly slice. Spread 5 or 6 slices on each sandwich, put on the tops, and enjoy!

**PREP TIME:** 10 minutes
**COOK TIME:** 25 to 30 minutes
**TOTAL TIME:** 35 to 40 minutes

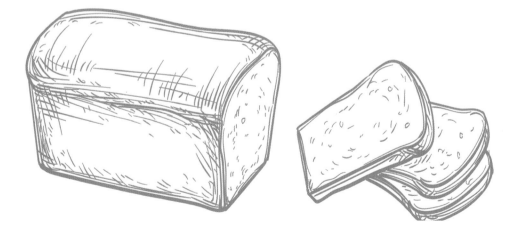

# QUICK, EASY GYROS

*I first discovered gyros several years back when I moved to Chicago for college—and I've been in love with them ever since. But making them isn't always so easy. I've made the meat from scratch and it was delicious, but I just don't have that kind of time every day! Using the Trader Joe's ingredients, however, I can whip them up as often as I want and barely add to the dish pile. It's a complete win in every way!*

**8 ounces Trader Joe's Gyro Slices**

**3 to 4 Roma tomatoes**

**1 white onion**

**4 pitas**

**Trader Joe's Tzatziki Creamy Garlic Cucumber Dip**

**2 cups chopped romaine**

**Trader Joe's Marinated Olive Duo with Lemon and Herbs**

**YIELD: 4 GYROS**

Lay out the gyro slices in the air fryer basket, not overlapping. Cook at 400°F for 3 minutes. Remove from the basket and lay on paper towels. Pat away the grease. Let stand while you chop tomatoes and onion.

Plate the pitas and spread on the tzatziki sauce, to taste (I typically use about 1 teaspoon per gyro). Next, layer in the veggies on the pitas. Finally, add the gyro slices and olives. Serve immediately.

**PREP TIME:** 5 to 7 minutes
**COOK TIME:** 3 minutes
**TOTAL TIME:** 8 to 10 minutes

# GYRO GRILLED CHEESE

*Looking for an easy, fun twist on that standard grilled cheese sandwich? Look no farther than this simple, gyro-inspired deliciousness!*

olive oil spray

8 slices wheat or French bread

8 slices cheddar cheese

1 (8-ounce) package Trader Joe's Gyro Slices

**YIELD: 4 SANDWICHES**

Spray the air fryer basket with olive oil spray, then preheat the air fryer to 350°F. Place four slices of bread on a plate, then layer on one slice of cheese, 2 gyro slices, then another slice of cheese. Place a second piece of bread on the meat-cheese stack. Then place each sandwich in the air fryer, lightly spraying with a thin layer of olive oil spray.

Cook for 3 to 4 minutes, then flip the sandwich and cook for an additional 2 to 3 minutes. Remove from the air fryer and let stand for 2 to 3 minutes before serving.

**PREP TIME:** 5 minutes
**COOK TIME:** 5 to 7 minutes
**TOTAL TIME:** 10 to 12 minutes

# HASH BROWN GRILLED CHEESE

*I love grilled cheese, so finding a twist to make them a little different always makes me happy. At the suggestion of a friend, I tried out the hash brown sandwich idea and loved it! Hopefully you will, too. I mean, it's hash browns, cheese, and Canadian bacon. You can't really go wrong with that combo!*

olive oil spray

1 pound 6.5 ounces (1 package) Trader Joe's Hashbrowns, frozen

5 slices cheddar or Colby cheese

5 slices Canadian bacon

**YIELD: 5 SANDWICHES**

Spray the basket of your air fryer with olive oil, then preheat to 400°F. While that's heating up, lightly spray the hash browns with olive oil. Layer 1 slice of cheese and 1 slice of Canadian bacon between each pair of hash browns, making 5 sandwiches.

Cook the sandwiches for 7 to 10 minutes. The hash browns should be golden-brown and crispy. Remove from the basket and let stand 3 to 5 minutes before serving.

**PREP TIME:** 5 minutes
**COOK TIME:** 7 to 10 minutes
**TOTAL TIME:** 12 to 15 minutes

# VEGGIE QUESADILLAS

*Quesadillas make for a quick, easy, and delicious meal that practically anyone can love. This particular version is great for sharing with my vegetarian friends, too.*

**olive oil spray**

**4 large flour tortillas**

**½ cup Trader Joe's Dairy Free Mozzarella Style Shreds**

**1 large red bell pepper, thinly sliced**

**1 cup Trader Joe's Organic Black Beans**

**2 teaspoons Trader Joe's Chile Lime Seasoning Blend**

**½ cup drained Trader Joe's Mild Pico de Gallo Salsa**

**YIELD: 4 QUESADILLAS**

Lightly spray the air fryer basket with olive oil, then preheat the air fryer to 400°F. Place the tortillas on a flat, dry surface. Sprinkle half the cheese divided evenly across the 4 tortillas, covering only one half of each, then layer the veggies and beans. Finish by sprinkling the remainder of the cheese on top of the veggies and about ½ teaspoon of the seasoning blend over each quesadilla, then fold the tortillas over the filling.

Carefully place each quesadilla in the air fryer basket and cook for 5 minutes. Using tongs or spatula, flip the quesadillas and cook for another 5 minutes.

Remove from the air fryer, plate, and serve with pico de gallo.

**PREP TIME:** 5 minutes
**COOK TIME:** 10 minutes
**TOTAL TIME:** 15 minutes

# BUFFALO SALMON SANDWICHES

*Okay, so I gotta confess something. Much as I love sushi, I'm still not much of a fish person. I first decided to tolerate salmon one night when I was babysitting and that was literally the only gluten-free food available to me. I've found some alternative ways to enjoy salmon and other fish, but a strong sauce and loads of goodies to accompany it is usually the way to win me over. These Buffalo salmon sandwiches are a direct result of that desire to add more healthy fish that I can love.*

olive oil spray

2 salmon fillets, approximately 4 ounces each

1 tablespoon Buffalo wing sauce

4 slices Trader Joe's Sprouted Wheat Sourdough Bread

Trader Joe's Chunky Blue Cheese Dressing & Dip

red onion slices, to taste

romaine, to taste

**YIELD: 2 SANDWICHES**

Lightly spray the air fryer basket, then preheat the air fryer to 400°F for 5 minutes. While that's heating up, lay the salmon fillets out on a baking sheet. Remove any skin from the fish, then, using a basting brush, coat the salmon with Buffalo sauce on all sides. Place the salmon in the basket and cook for 7 to 10 minutes or until it reaches an internal temperature of 145°F. Remove the fish from the basket and let cool while you prepare the sandwiches.

Plate the bread. Lightly spread blue cheese dressing on all 4 slices, then lay a stack of onion and lettuce on 2 of the slices. Place the salmon on the stacked slices of bread and close with the other slices. Serve immediately.

**PREP TIME:** 7 minutes
**COOK TIME:** 7 to 10 minutes
**TOTAL TIME:** 14 to 17 minutes

# HAM, CHEESE, AND EGGPLANT SANDWICHES

*I absolutely adore eggplant. I also adore ham and cheese sandwiches—hot or cold. When I came across TJ's eggplant with tomato and onion, I got inspired...and this is the result.*

**softened unsalted butter**

**8 slices Trader Joe's Multigrain Bread**

**8 slices of Colby Jack cheese**

**1 (9.9-ounce) container Trader Joe's Grecian Style Eggplant with Tomatoes & Onions**

**11 to 14 ounces premium ham**

**YIELD: 4 SANDWICHES**

Add a light coat of butter to 1 side of each slice of bread. Place the buttered side down in the air fryer basket, then build the sandwich with 1 slice of cheese on each bread slice, a layer of eggplant with the accompanying sauce, tomatoes, and onions, then the ham, then another slice of cheese. Finally, top each stack with another slice of bread, with the buttered side out.

Cook in the air fryer at 360°F for 5 minutes. Carefully flip the sandwich over and cook for another 5 minutes. Remove from the air fryer and serve immediately.

**PREP TIME:** 5 minutes
**COOK TIME:** 10 minutes
**TOTAL TIME:** 15 minutes

# RED PEPPER GRILLED CHEESE AND BACON SANDWICHES

*A tangy sandwich is always welcome in our house. A tangy cheese with some bacon? Even more welcome.*

**4 strips Trader Joe's Uncured Apple Smoked Bacon**

**softened unsalted butter**

**8 slices Trader Joe's Multigrain Bread**

**8 slices cheddar cheese**

**Trader Joe's Red Pepper Spread with Eggplant & Garlic**

**YIELD: 4 SANDWICHES**

Place the bacon strips in a single layer in the air fryer basket and cook at 350°F for 7 minutes or until the bacon is browned and halfway crisp. Remove the bacon and place it on a paper towel-lined plate to drain.

While the bacon is draining and cooling, butter 1 side of each slice of bread. Place 4 slices of bread, buttered-side down in the air fryer basket. Add a slice of cheddar cheese to each slice of bread. Slather some of the red pepper spread onto each slice. Once the bacon has cooled enough to handle, use your hands to crumble it into small pieces. Then evenly sprinkle the bacon on the sandwich stacks on top of the cheese. Then add another slice of cheese, then top with the other slices of bread, buttered-side up.

Cook for 5 minutes, then carefully flip the sandwiches. Cook for another 5 minutes. Remove from the air fryer and serve immediately.

**PREP TIME:** 7 minutes
**COOK TIME:** 10 minutes
**TOTAL TIME:** 17 minutes

# CAPRESE GRILLED CHEESE SANDWICHES

*I'm always looking for interesting twists on grilled cheese—and I adore Italian foods. This idea of a Caprese salad turned grilled cheese seemed like the perfect marriage.*

**8 slices Trader Joe's Sliced French Brioche**

**4 tablespoons Trader Joe's Vegan Kale, Cashew & Basil Pesto**

**1 (8-ounce) container Trader Joe's All Natural Ciliegine Whole Milk Fresh Mozzarella**

**1 to 2 large tomatoes, sliced**

**softened unsalted butter**

**YIELD: 4 SANDWICHES**

Preheat your air fryer to 350°F. While that's heating up, lay out all 8 slices of bread on a clean, dry surface or platter. Spread ½ tablespoon of pesto on each slice of bread, then place chunks of the mozzarella onto 4 of the slices of bread. (I like 2 per sandwich, you can use less or more—whatever you're feeling!) Next, layer on the tomato slices. Close the sandwiches.

Now lightly butter both sides of each sandwich and place them in the air fryer basket. Cook for 6 to 8 minutes or until the cheese completely melts. Remove from air fryer, plate, and serve immediately.

**PREP TIME:** 5 minutes
**COOK TIME:** 6 to 8 minutes
**TOTAL TIME:** 11 to 13 minutes

# TURKEY AND BRIE PUFF PASTRY SANDWICHES

*For a different twist on the grilled cheese, I present you the puff pastry turkey and brie sandwich. So fast, delicious, and utterly easy!*

**1 (18.3-ounce) package Trader Joe's All Butter Puff Pastry**

**1 large egg yolk, lightly beaten**

**Deli sliced turkey**

**Trader Joe's Triple Creme Brie Cheese**

**YIELD: 4 SANDWICHES**

Preheat the air fryer to 350°F. Lay out the pastry sheets and brush the egg yolk along both of the longer sides of the pastries. Cut each sheet into quarters. Center equal portions of the turkey and brie into 4 pieces of pastry. Cover each with the other pieces of pastry and pinch the edges together all around.

Line a baking sheet with parchment paper and set the sandwiches on the sheet. Place in the air fryer and cook for 15 to 20 minutes or until the pastry turns golden-brown. Remove and let cool for 5 minutes before serving.

**PREP TIME:** 10 minutes
**COOK TIME:** 15 to 20 minutes
**TOTAL TIME:** 25 to 30 minutes

# FRIED EGG AND TOMATO SANDWICHES

*One of the great, simple food pleasures in life is a fried egg sandwich. I love these any time of day, for any occasion. When I discovered Trader Joe's pepper jelly, though, the game was upped and I had to meet it with these tasty, simple sandwiches that are absolutely to die for. Enjoy!*

olive oil spray

4 large eggs

salt and pepper, to taste

8 slices Trader Joe's Sourdough Wheat Bread

4 teaspoons Trader Joe's Hot & Sweet Pepper Jelly

4 large-circumference tomato slices

4 slices Trader Joe's New Zealand Organic Sliced Cheddar Cheese

**YIELD: 4 SANDWICHES**

Preheat the air fryer to 350°F for 5 minutes. While that's heating up, grab some aluminum foil and a biscuit cutter or a Mason jar lid. Spray the foil with olive oil spray, then fold up around the biscuit cutter or lid as your egg mold. Then crack the egg into the mold and season lightly with salt and pepper, to taste. Repeat with the remaining eggs, using a total of 4 molds.

Place the egg mold(s) in the air fryer basket and cook for 4 minutes. Gently flip the eggs with a spatula and cook for another 4 minutes. While the eggs are cooking, toast the bread and then plate. Spread the pepper jelly on 1 slice of bread per sandwich (both, if you love the jelly like I do!), then place the eggs on the saucy slices. Layer on tomato slices and cheese, then top with the other bread slices. Serve immediately.

**PREP TIME:** 5 minutes
**COOK TIME:** 8 minutes
**TOTAL TIME:** 13 minutes

# BBTS

*The first time I ever had brie was when I was sitting at a train station in Paris, waiting for a connection to Madrid. I have no idea what took me so long to enjoy this amazing, soft cheese, but now I use it whenever I can on anything and everything. And if you've never had a bacon brie tomato sandwich, I'll give you a few minutes to regain yourself after entering this heaven.*

**8 strips bacon**

**8 slices of bread**

**4 tomato slices**

**lettuce leaves**

**½ wedge Trader Joe's Triple Creme Brie Cheese, cut into 4 to 8 slices**

**YIELD: 4 SANDWICHES**

Preheat air fryer to 350°F. Place the bacon strips in a single layer in the air fryer basket and cook for 7 minutes or until the bacon is browned and halfway crisp. Remove the bacon and place on a paper towel-lined plate to drain.

While the bacon is draining, place 4 slices of bread on a flat surface. Layer on the tomato, lettuce, and brie. Place the bacon onto the brie and then cover the sandwiches with the other bread slices. Place the sandwich on a small baking sheet and cook for 3 to 5 minutes in the air fryer. Remove and serve immediately.

**PREP TIME:** 7 minutes
**COOK TIME:** 10 to 15 minutes
**TOTAL TIME:** 17 to 22 minutes

# FRIED CHICKEN SANDWICHES

*I grew up in the South and worked at Chick-fil-A for some of my just-post-college years. I know a thing or two about fried chicken sandwiches. Combining that knowledge with the amazing ingredients at TJ's, though, has upped my game on this front—especially with that focaccia! Hopefully you'll enjoy this easy, quick meal as much as my hubby does.*

olive oil spray

**4 Trader Joe's Breaded Chicken Tenderloin Breasts, frozen**

**1 loaf Trader Joe's Focaccia Bread Roasted Tomato & Parmesan, cut into quarters and halved**

**8 teaspoons Trader Joe's Hot & Sweet Pepper Jelly**

**4 slices mozzarella cheese**

**YIELD: 4 SANDWICHES**

Preheat the air fryer to 375°F. Lightly spray the air fryer basket with olive oil spray, then place the chicken breasts inside. Cook for 7 minutes, then flip with tongs and cook for another 7 minutes. The chicken should be soft and pliable when done.

While the chicken's cooking, place your focaccia bread on plates. Spread about 1 teaspoon of pepper jelly on each slice of bread, then place 1 slice of mozzarella cheese on 4 of the bread slices. Remove the chicken from the air fryer and place 1 breast each immediately on the cheese slices. Press the other slices of bread onto the chicken and let stand for 5 minutes before serving.

**PREP TIME:** 5 minutes
**COOK TIME:** 14 minutes
**TOTAL TIME:** 19 minutes

# Chapter 12

# DECADENT DELIGHTS

# APRICOT CAKE DOUGHNUTS

*I'm a huge fan of cake doughnuts, but being gluten free, there aren't that many flavor options (if any) available out there. When I spotted the organic apricot preserves for the first time, my immediate thought was, Can I make apricot doughnuts? The answer, of course, was yes!*

**FOR THE DOUGHNUTS**

2¼ cups Trader Joe's Gluten Free All Purpose Flour

1 teaspoon baking soda

¼ cup almond flour

½ teaspoon salt

1 large egg, room temperature

⅓ cup cane sugar

¼ cup milk

olive oil spray

½ cup Trader Joe's Organic Apricot Preserves

2 tablespoons unsalted butter, melted

olive oil

**FOR THE CINNAMON SUGAR GLAZE**

1 stick of butter (8 tablespoons), melted

1 tablespoon ground cinnamon

2 tablespoons cane sugar

**YIELD: 16 DOUGHNUTS**

In a large bowl, whisk together the flour, baking soda, almond flour, and salt. In a separate, smaller bowl, beat the egg for 2 minutes, then add in the sugar, milk, apricot preserves, and melted butter. Pour the wet ingredients into the bowl with the flour mixture and beat together until thoroughly combined.

If the dough is excessively sticky, add additional flour, 1 tablespoon at a time, until the dough reaches a sticky cookie dough consistency. Cover and chill for 1 to 2 hours. After the dough has chilled, pull it out and set aside.

On a clean, flat, dry surface sprinkle some flour evenly. Take out a portion of the dough about 1/16th of total and first roll it into a ball, then roll it out into a fat rope, about 6 inches long. Be sure not to get too much flour on the dough, or it will dry out while cooking. Bring the ends together and pinch to close them into a circle. Repeat with the remainder of the dough.

Preheat the air fryer for 5 minutes to 350°F. Lightly spray the inside of the basket with olive oil, then carefully lay as many doughnuts in the basket as you can without the doughnuts touching. Cook for 5 minutes. Repeat until doughnuts are all cooked.

While the doughnuts are cooking, make your cinnamon glaze by combining the melted butter, cinnamon, and sugar in a small, shallow bowl. With a spoon, mix until thoroughly combined.

Remove the doughnuts from the basket with tongs and immediately plunge them into cinnamon sugar glaze. Thoroughly coat all sides (I use a spoon to get those rounded edges), then set aside on a plate to cool and dry. Wait an hour or two before serving so that the glaze has time to set.

**PREP TIME:** 30 to 40 minutes
**COOK TIME:** 5 minutes each round, approximately 4 rounds total
**REST TIME:** 1 to 2 hours
**TOTAL TIME:** 1 hour 35 minutes to 3 hours

# WATERMELON DOUGHNUT HOLES

*I'd never heard of watermelon-flavored doughnuts before, so I admit, when the idea first popped into my head to make doughnut holes with Trader Joe's watermelon fruit spread, I was a little surprised at myself. It sounded so...odd. But, also, oddly delicious. So, when I whipped these up, I was both surprised and not-so-surprised at how absolutely delightful they are.*

**2 cups flour**

**1 teaspoon baking soda**

**olive oil**

**¼ cup almond flour**

**½ teaspoon salt**

**1 large egg, room temperature**

**⅓ cup cane sugar**

**¼ cup milk**

**½ cup Trader Joe's Organic Watermelon Fruit Spread**

**2 tablespoons unsalted butter, melted**

**YIELD: 35 TO 40 DOUGHNUT HOLES**

In a large mixing bowl, whisk together the flour, baking soda, almond flour, and salt. In a separate medium bowl, beat together the egg, sugar, milk, fruit spread, and melted butter until thoroughly combined. Pour the wet ingredients into the bowl with the flour mixture and beat together until thoroughly combined. Cover and chill for 1 hour. After the dough has chilled, pull it out and set aside.

Preheat air fryer to 350°F. Spray the air fryer basket lightly with olive oil. Sprinkle a teaspoon of flour over a clean, flat, dry surface. Remove the dough from the bowl and gently knead for 2 minutes, then separate it into equal portions, about 35 to 40 total. In your hands, roll each portion into a ball, then place them into your air fryer, not touching one another. Cook for 3 minutes, remove with tongs, and let cool completely before rolling in powdered sugar. Repeat with the remaining doughnut holes, until all are cooked, cooled, and coated. Serve with some milk for best results.

**PREP TIME:** 20 to 30 minutes
**COOK TIME:** 3 minutes each round, approximately 3 rounds total
**REST TIME:** 1 hour
**TOTAL TIME:** 1 hour 23 minutes to 1 hour 39 minutes

# GLUTEN-FREE FIG BARS

*So, I love fig bars, but almost no one makes them gluten free. I figured, well, homemade is healthier anyway since you can control the amount of sugar and know exactly what goes into them. And Trader Joe's fig butter is amazing. So, why not? These are now one of our absolute favorite desserts in the world. Perfect for game nights, dinner parties, and special occasions.*

⅔ cup cane or white sugar

⅓ cup brown sugar, packed

½ cup unsalted butter, softened

1 tablespoon milk

2 teaspoons vanilla extract

3½ cups almond flour

1 teaspoon baking powder

½ teaspoon salt

gluten-free all-purpose flour

1 (11-ounce) jar Trader Joe's Fig Butter

**YIELD: 12 FIG BARS**

In a large mixing bowl with a hand mixer, cream together the sugar, brown sugar, and butter until the mixture is evenly combined, about 3 minutes. No sugar should remain at the bottom of the bowl. Add in the milk and vanilla and mix again until smooth, about 2 minutes. In a separate medium mixing bowl, whisk together the almond flour, baking powder, and salt.

Pour the dry mixture into the butter mixture and blend thoroughly until completely combined and smooth. Cover the bowl and chill for 1 hour.

Sprinkle some gluten-free all-purpose flour on a clean, flat, dry surface. Preheat the air fryer to 400°F for 5 minutes. Divide the dough in half and set aside 1 half. Using your fingers, evenly spread the first half of the dough out into the bottom of a greased and lightly floured 9 x 9-inch baking pan, or 2 smaller baking pans if that won't fit into your air fryer. Spread out until you have a fairly even layer of dough. Next, spread the entire contents of the jar of fig butter across the dough. Now take the second half of the dough and break it into smaller lumps. Space them evenly across the pan and spread them out across the fig butter layer, pressing out and around to create the top crust of the fig bars.

Cook for 10 minutes. Remove from the air fryer and let cool in the pan. Then cut the bars evenly and enjoy!

**PREP TIME:** 15 to 20 minutes
**COOK TIME:** 10 minutes
**REST TIME:** 1 hour
**TOTAL TIME:** 1 hour 25 minutes to 1 hour 30 minutes

# THUMBPRINT COOKIES WITH LEMON CURD FILLING

*Thumbprint cookies were one of those goodies I could help make when I was small. Perhaps a love for these jammy delights has stayed with me because of this—or maybe it's just because they're so darn delicious! For this particular recipe, I use my absolute favorite dessert flavoring: lemon curd. If you're a lemon lover like me, you're going to adore these!*

1 cup unsalted butter, softened

⅔ cup cane sugar

2 large egg yolks

1 teaspoon vanilla extract

¼ teaspoon salt

2⅓ cups Trader Joe's Gluten Free All Purpose Flour

½ cup Trader Joe's Lemon Curd

**YIELD: 24 COOKIES**

In a large mixing bowl, combine the butter and sugar, creaming together with a hand mixer until they're well incorporated. Then add in the egg yolks, vanilla, and salt. Mix in thoroughly. Finally, add in the flour and beat with the hand mixer until the dough has "dried up."

At this point, grab a wooden spoon and use it to finish mixing together the dough. The dough will remain a bit crumbly until the very end. When you can press it together easily with the wooden spoon and all the flour is absorbed, the dough is ready.

Preheat the air fryer to 350°F for 5 minutes. Now take about a tablespoon of dough and pat together with your hands. When the dough becomes supple after a few seconds, roll it into a ball and place on a pan lined with parchment paper or silicone. Repeat with the remaining dough. Once all the balls are laid out, gently press your thumb into each cookie, leaving a small impression. Spoon 1 teaspoon of lemon curd into each divot. Cook for 3 minutes. If the cookies aren't lightly brown around the edges, cook for an additional 2 to 3 minutes.

Remove from the pan and cool on a cooling rack for 10 minutes before serving.

**PREP TIME:** 10 to 13 minutes
**COOK TIME:** 5 to 6 minutes
**TOTAL TIME:** 15 to 19 minutes

# MATCHA MOCHI FRIED ICE CREAM

*I'll warn you—these have to be made precisely or they'll fail. Despite being super easy to make, they're not so easy to execute. That dough has to wrap completely around the ice cream, that temperature has to be precise, you really do need to freeze the balls that long ahead of time, and you can't add a minute more to the cooking time. Despite all that, after you make them a time or two, you'll have the hang of it—and, even if they melt, they still taste amazing.*

**1 cup Trader Joe's Matcha Green Tea Ice Cream**

**olive oil spray**

**2 tablespoons matcha powder**

**2 cups glutinous rice flour**

**½ cup cane sugar**

**2 cups water**

**¼ cup tapioca or cornstarch**

**6 tablespoons Trader Joe's Fleur de Sel Caramel Sauce, divided**

**YIELD: 12 MOCHI**

Scoop out ice cream and form into approximately 1-tablespoon balls. Wrap balls individually in plastic wrap and refreeze for 4 hours.

Spray olive oil into the inside of a large, microwave-safe ceramic or glass container, going up the sides. Now dump in the matcha, glutinous rice flour, and sugar. Mix up with a fork until well incorporated, then add the water. Mix thoroughly. The blend will be very liquidy. Cook the mixture on high in the microwave for 3 minutes and 30 seconds.

Heavily dust a clean, flat surface with about ¼ cup tapioca or cornstarch. With a spoon, remove the rice dough from the bowl and place it on the starch-covered surface. Sprinkle a little more starch onto the dough and work it into the dough a little so that you can safely handle it.

Once you can comfortably handle the dough, pinch off approximately 2-tablespoon pieces and shape roughly into balls. Use a spoon to flatten the balls and dust with more starch, as needed.

Once all the dough has been shaped into flattened disks, remove the ice cream balls from the freezer and unwrap quickly (one at a time). Place in the dough disks, fold up the disks around them and pinch the tops closed. Ensure that the dough is solid all the way around and completely encompasses the ice cream, or it will melt!

Place the ice creams into silicone cupcake liners and then place the liners in the air fryer. (If you need to do multiple rounds to cook, place the mochi balls in the freezer to keep cold.)

Cook the mochi balls at 175°F for 2 to 3 minutes. Remove quickly and spoon ½ tablespoon of caramel sauce into each liner and serve immediately.

**PREP TIME:** 15 minutes
**COOK TIME:** 2 to 3 minutes
**REST TIME:** 4 hours
**TOTAL TIME:** 4 hours, 17 to 18 minutes

# ALMOND FRIED ICE CREAM

*Much like the mochi fried ice cream balls, the fried ice cream has to be made precisely or you'll wind up with melted blobs of ice cream and almond flour. I recommend reading through the directions a few times before making the dessert. Then enjoy! (And, even if they fail, they taste amazing. I know. Mine failed the first three attempts.)*

**1 cup Trader Joe's French Vanilla Ice Cream**

**2 tablespoons almond flour**

**2 tablespoons breadcrumbs**

**1 tablespoon all-purpose flour**

**1 tablespoon almond slices**

**2 tablespoons Panko breadcrumbs**

**½ teaspoon ground cinnamon**

**1 egg white**

**½ to 1 teaspoon Trader Joe's Fleur de Sel Caramel Sauce**

**YIELD: 10 TO 12 ICE CREAM BALLS**

Scoop out ice cream and form into approximately 1 tablespoon-sized balls. Wrap balls individually in plastic wrap and refreeze for 4 hours. Shortly before pulling the ice cream balls out of the freezer, in a small bowl mix together the dry ingredients with a fork or whisk. Put the egg white in a separate small, shallow bowl.

Once the ice cream balls are rock solid, pull them out of the freezer. For each ball, unwrap quickly, roll in egg white, then transfer to the dry mix. Make sure to thoroughly coat the ice cream balls with both layers. Then place them in silicone baking cups and set in the air fryer basket (do not preheat).

Once all the ice cream balls are coated and ready, cook for 2 to 3 minutes at 175°F. Remove immediately from the air fryer and top each with ½ to 1 teaspoon of caramel sauce. Serve immediately.

**PREP TIME:** 10 minutes
**COOK TIME:** 2 to 3 minutes
**REST TIME:** 4 hours
**TOTAL TIME:** 4 hours, 12 to 13 minutes

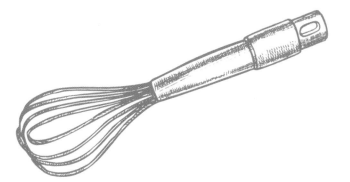

# TOASTED CHOCOLATE PEANUT BUTTER MOCHI BALLS

*Since I absolutely adore the mochi dough and could eat it all day, I decided to have a little fun and experiment. Powdery delights like matcha and cocoa blend seamlessly into the dough, so that got me thinking: peanut butter cups. And who doesn't like TJ's? I had to try it! The result: amazing!*

olive oil spray

1 tablespoon plus 1 teaspoon unsweetened cocoa powder, divided

2 cups glutinous rice flour

½ cup cane sugar

2 cups water

¼ cup cornstarch

12 Trader Joe's Milk Chocolate Peanut Butter Cups

12 teaspoons Trader Joe's Fleur de Sel Caramel Sauce, divided

**YIELD: 12 MOCHI BALLS**

Spray olive oil into the inside of a large, microwave-safe ceramic or glass container, going up the sides. Now dump in 1 tablespoon cocoa powder, glutinous rice flour, and sugar together. Mix with a fork until well incorporated, then add the water. Mix thoroughly. The blend will be very liquidy. Cook the mixture in the microwave on high for 3 minutes and 30 seconds.

Heavily dust a clean, flat surface with about ¼ cup cornstarch and 1 teaspoon cocoa powder. With a spoon, remove the rice dough from the bowl and place on the starch-covered surface. Sprinkle a little more cornstarch onto the dough and work into the dough a little so that you can safely handle it.

Once you can comfortably handle the dough, pinch off approximately 2 tablespoons of dough and shape roughly into balls. Use a spoon to flatten the balls and dust with more starch, as needed.

Once all the dough has been shaped into flattened disks, place 1 peanut butter cup into each disk. Fold the disk up and around the candy and pinch closed. Make sure the dough completely encompasses the candy to avoid melting the candy too much.

Place the mochi into silicone cupcake liners and then place the liners in the air fryer.

Cook the mochi balls at 175°F for 3 to 5 minutes (do not preheat). Remove quickly and chill for 1 hour, then spoon about 1 teaspoon of caramel sauce onto each mochi before serving.

**PREP TIME:** 15 minutes
**COOK TIME:** 6½ minutes to 8½ minutes
**REST TIME:** 1 hour
**TOTAL TIME:** 1 hour 21½ minutes to 1 hour 23½ minutes

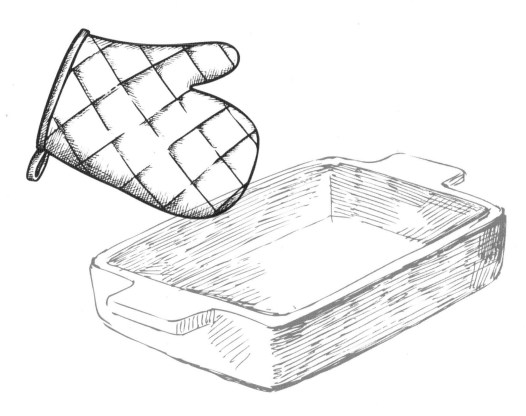

# BAKED BRIE AND BERRY BUNS

*One of my favorite light dinners has always been fruit, nuts, and cheese. When I discovered brie, that upped my game. And then I discovered the air fryer and premade pastry dough. Now these are going to be added to our annual Christmas buffet.*

**1 (18.3-ounce) package Trader Joe's All Butter Puff Pastry**

**¼ cup Trader Joe's Organic Reduced Sugar Cherry Preserves**

**1 wedge Trader Joe's Triple Creme Brie Cheese**

**olive oil spray**

**YIELD: 12 BUNS**

Preheat the air fryer to 400°F. While that's heating up, roll out the puff pastry dough on a flat surface. Use a rolling pin to flatten a little more to ¼-inch thickness, if needed. Cut each sheet into sixths. At the center of each piece, place a small chunk of brie and a teaspoon of cherry preserves. Fold the dough up around the filling and pinch at the center to close.

Spray the inside of the air fryer basket, then carefully place the buns inside the basket, not touching one another, and then cook for 10 to 12 minutes or until the dough is crispy, golden-brown. Remove from the air fryer and let cool completely before serving.

**PREP TIME:** 15 minutes
**COOK TIME:** 10 to 12 minutes
**TOTAL TIME:** 25 to 27 minutes

# EASY APPLE CRISP

*This is one of the absolute easiest dessert recipes I make. You literally just dump everything into a pan, cook, and serve in a bowl with a little bit of almond milk. Amazing every time.*

**coconut oil spray**

**2 large Granny Smith apples**

**2 cups Trader Joe's Organic Fruit & Seed Granola**

**½ cup unsweetened applesauce**

**2 teaspoons ground cinnamon**

**1 teaspoon vanilla extract**

**1 cup almond milk, divided**

**YIELD: 4 SERVINGS**

Preheat the air fryer to 400°F. Lightly spray an air fryer pan with coconut oil. Then combine all ingredients, except the almond milk, in the pan. Cook for 15 minutes. Remove from the air fryer and immediately dish out into 4 small, shallow bowls. Pour ¼ cup of almond milk into each bowl. Let sit for 3 to 4 minutes and enjoy!

**PREP TIME:** 5 minutes
**COOK TIME:** 15 minutes
**TOTAL TIME:** 20 minutes

# CINNAMON CARAMEL APPLE CHIPS

*A few years ago, I discovered Aldi's apple chips which, unfortunately, are only available for a small window each year. But thanks to my air fryer, I can make my own easily and quickly, whenever I want. And, to top that, enjoy them with Trader Joe's amazing Caramel sauce! (My favorite for making these is Honeycrisp or Granny Smith)*

**3 large, firm apples**

**ground cinnamon**

**Trader Joe's Fleur de Sel Caramel Sauce**

**YIELD: 3 TO 4 LARGE SERVINGS**

Thoroughly wash and dry your apples then core them and remove all seeds. Slice the apple as thinly as you can, aiming for about ⅛-inch thickness. A great way to manage this is with a mandoline or a super-sharp knife.

Preheat your air fryer to 390°F. While that's heating up, rub cinnamon on the apple slices. If you want lots of cinnamon, make sure every inch is covered. If you're looking for more of a "tinge" of cinnamon, lightly rubbing it on will be sufficient.

Lay as many apple slices in the air fryer basket as you can with none overlapping. Cook the slices for 4 minutes, then flip them over with tongs and cook for another 4 minutes. If you want the slices extra crunchy, add 1-minute increments of cooking time until the slices reach the crispness you're looking for. Repeat with the remaining apple slices.

Let the chips cool completely, then serve with the caramel sauce.

**PREP TIME:** 15 minutes
**COOK TIME:** 8 to 12 minutes
**TOTAL TIME:** 23 to 27 minutes

# GLUTEN-FREE PISTACHIO BROWNIES

*Here's a tasty, nutty, gluten-free delight the whole family can enjoy. I personally love the pistachios in this recipe, but if you prefer walnuts, pecans, or almond slices, you can easily replace the pistachios with them.*

½ cup gluten-free all-purpose flour

¼ cup Trader Joe's Cocoa Powder Unsweetened

¼ teaspoon salt

¼ cup almond milk

1 large egg

1 teaspoon vanilla extract

1 tablespoon ground flaxseed

½ cup shelled pistachios

**YIELD: 12 BROWNIES**

In a medium mixing bowl, mix the flour, cocoa, and salt until thoroughly blended. Add in the almond milk, egg, vanilla, and flaxseed and mix again, until thoroughly blended. Now add the pistachios and mix thoroughly.

Preheat your air fryer to 350°F. While that's heating up, lightly grease an air fryer cake pan. Pour the batter into the pan and cook for 20 minutes. Test for doneness using a toothpick. If it doesn't come out clean, cook for an additional 2 to 3 minutes and test again. Repeat, as needed. When the brownies are done, remove the pan from the air fryer and let cool completely before cutting into squares and serving.

**PREP TIME:** 10 minutes
**COOK TIME:** 20 minutes
**TOTAL TIME:** 30 minutes

# FRIED JOE-JOE'S SLIMS

*I've never been much for deep-fried foods, despite growing up in the South. So, when I witnessed one of my best friends enjoying deep-fried Oreos at a sushi restaurant in St. Louis, I was intrigued. The idea seemed strange, for sure. But when it came time to prep the recipes for this cookbook, I thought, Why not take the concept and run with it with Joe-Joe's? My husband was skeptical at first, but then he bit in.*

**1 (8-ounce) package Trader Joe's Crescent Rolls dough**

**8 teaspoons Trader Joe's Fudge Sauce**

**16 Trader Joe's Joe-Joe's Slims**

**powdered sugar, for dusting (optional)**

**YIELD: 8 SERVINGS**

Preheat the air fryer to 350°F. While that's heating up, spread out the crescent roll dough on a flat, dry surface. Press down on the perforations to "seal" the seams. Cut the dough into 8 pieces. Slather 1 teaspoon of fudge sauce on each piece, then place 2 stacked Joe-Joe's in the center of each piece of dough. Fold up the dough around the cookies, being sure not to stretch the dough too thin.

Gently place the dough-wrapped cookies in the air fryer basket, not touching one another. Cook for 5 to 6 minutes or until the wraps are golden-brown. Remove with tongs and let cool. If desired, dust with powdered sugar, then serve.

**PREP TIME:** 7 minutes
**COOK TIME:** 5 to 6 minutes
**TOTAL TIME:** 12 to 13 minutes

# TRADER JOE'S ALMOND FLOUR CHOCOLATE CHIP COOKIES

*Easy, delicious and gluten free? Oh, you better believe I was going to teach you how to make these in an air fryer!*

1 (9.4-ounce) package Trader Joe's Almond Flour Chocolate Chip Baking Mix

3 tablespoons olive oil

2 teaspoons vanilla extract

3 tablespoons almond milk

**YIELD: 10 TO 12 COOKIES**

Preheat the air fryer to 350°F for 5 minutes. While that's heating up, mix the dough as the recipe on the package directs, but use olive oil and almond milk for those items. (They just taste better and are slightly healthier.) Make sure the dough is a little sticky by the time you're done.

Put parchment paper on the baking sheet and dollop out the dough in overflowing tablespoons. Cook for 3 to 5 minutes.

Let the cookies stand on the sheet for 1 to 2 minutes, then remove and let cool the rest of the way on a cooling rack.

**PREP TIME:** 5 minutes
**COOK TIME:** 3 to 5 minutes
**TOTAL TIME:** 8 to 10 minutes

# CONVERSIONS

## VOLUME

| U.S. | U.S. Equivalent | Metric |
|---|---|---|
| 1 tablespoon (3 teaspoons) | ½ fluid ounce | 15 milliliters |
| ¼ cup | 2 fluid ounces | 60 milliliters |
| ⅓ cup | 3 fluid ounces | 90 milliliters |
| ½ cup | 4 fluid ounces | 120 milliliters |
| ⅔ cup | 5 fluid ounces | 150 milliliters |
| ¾ cup | 6 fluid ounces | 180 milliliters |
| 1 cup | 8 fluid ounces | 240 milliliters |
| 2 cups | 16 fluid ounces | 480 milliliters |

## WEIGHT

| U.S. | Metric |
|---|---|
| ½ ounce | 15 grams |
| 1 ounce | 30 grams |
| 2 ounces | 60 grams |
| ¼ pound | 115 grams |
| ⅓ pound | 150 grams |
| ½ pound | 225 grams |
| ¾ pound | 350 grams |
| 1 pound | 450 grams |

## TEMPERATURE

| Fahrenheit (°F) | Celsius (°C) | Fahrenheit (°F) | Celsius (°C) |
|---|---|---|---|
| 70°F | 20°C | 220°F | 105°C |
| 100°F | 40°C | 240°F | 115°C |
| 120°F | 50°C | 260°F | 125°C |
| 130°F | 55°C | 280°F | 140°C |
| 140°F | 60°C | 300°F | 150°C |
| 150°F | 65°C | 325°F | 165°C |
| 160°F | 70°C | 350°F | 175°C |
| 170°F | 75°C | 375°F | 190°C |
| 180°F | 80°C | 400°F | 200°C |
| 190°F | 90°C | 425°F | 220°C |
| 200°F | 95°C | 450°F | 230°C |

# RECIPE INDEX

# ACKNOWLEDGMENTS

Sending out a giant thanks to my amazing friends and family who helped me along in the creation journey of this cookbook using Trader Joe's amazing ingredients. To my husband, thank you for being a happy guinea pig, even through the failures and overcooked meat. To my best friend, Amber Saldivar, thank you for introducing me to some of these TJ's products years back. Mom, thanks for your happy experimenting with me, as always. Thank you, Cyndi Lublink, for letting me process through ideas with you and your willingness to use your kitchen to experiment on recipes (even if I didn't hand over that many ahead of time).

And, of course, a giant thank you to Trader Joe's for providing us with some of the most flavorful, easy-to-use ingredients that make us feel better about life and the gluten-free way.

# ABOUT THE AUTHOR

Rita Mock-Pike is the granddaughter of aviatrix Jerrie Mock, the first woman to fly solo around the world. Rita is grateful for the many stories her grandmother shared and the encouragement she always supplied to her granddaughter to pursue her own dreams and adventures in life. Rita is a full-time journalist and content writer, part-time magician's assistant, and full-time grad student pursuing her master's in Christian Ministry. She's also the editor-in-chief of the *MockingOwl Roost*, a literary and art magazine welcoming new and seasoned writers and artists from across the globe. Rita lives in the greater Chicago area with her amazing husband, Matt, and the fluffy kitten queen, Lady Stardust.